THE BORDER COUNTRY
A WALKER'S GUIDE

The Five Steps of Dob's Linn

Good Walking
Alan Hall

THE BORDER COUNTRY
A WALKER'S GUIDE

53 Walks in the Border Hills
and the
Southern Uplands

by

ALAN HALL

CICERONE PRESS
MILNTHORPE, CUMBRIA

ISBN 1 85284 116 8

British Library Cataloguing-in-Publication Data. A catalogue record for this book is available from the British Library.

Dedicated to Greta

ACKNOWLEDGEMENTS

Special thanks to Greta my wife, who travelled with me every step of the way, from the book's conception to its completion. A shared journey that enlarged the pleasure and enhanced the outcome. Also included is our son Kevin, with his unbounded enthusiasm and energy for the entire project; his knowledgeable company on the hills lightened the step. I am deeply indebted to Hector Innes for his expert advice on matters photographic, to Roberta Carruthers for her charming illustrations and to Quentin McLaren, Countryside Development, Borders Regional Council, my appreciation for the information concerning local Rights of Way. Thanks also to my many friends who unearthed their ageing volumes rich in Borders history and legend, and finally to hill walkers well met along the way who spoke with pleasure of their time in the Borders. I offer this guide to all who have given me help and encouragement, and to all lovers of the Borderland, with sincere wishes that it stimulates you all to travel just that little bit further.

All photographs, maps and diagrams relating to the Borders are by the author.

CONTENTS

INTRODUCTION

(a) Background

(b) Action

CHAPTER 1: THE CHEVIOT HILLS

CHAPTER 4: THE TWEEDSMUIR HILLS

Advice to Readers

Readers are advised that whilst every effort is taken by the author to ensure the accuracy of this guidebook, changes can occur which may affect the contents. It is advisable to check locally on transport, accommodation, shops etc but even rights-of-way can be altered and, more especially overseas, paths can be eradicated by landslip, forest fires or changes of ownership.

The publisher would welcome notes of any such changes

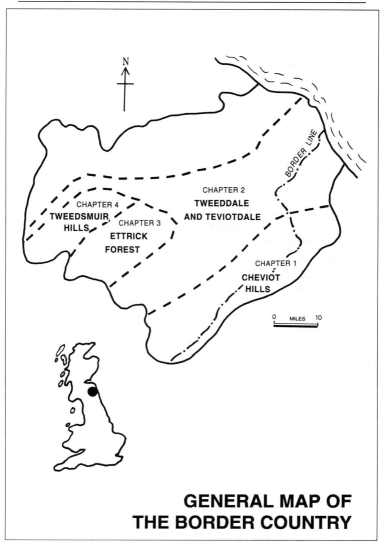

N

CHAPTER 2
**TWEEDDALE
AND TEVIOTDALE**

CHAPTER 4
**TWEEDSMUIR
HILLS**

CHAPTER 3
**ETTRICK
FOREST**

BORDER LINE

CHAPTER 1
**CHEVIOT
HILLS**

0   MILES   10

GENERAL MAP OF
THE BORDER COUNTRY

"Grey recumbent tombs of the dead in desert places,
Standing stones on the vacant wine-red moor,
Hills of sheep, and the homes of the silent vanquished races,
And winds, austere and pure."

R.L. Stevenson

Introduction

BACKGROUND

THE BORDER HILLS AND SOUTHERN UPLANDS

Four graphic lines encapsulate the solitude that lies between England and Scotland. An upland area which, though neglected by rambler and mountain walker alike, can offer both a wealth of adventure.

The area, though linked to the North of England and the Lothians of Scotland has, by its geographical seclusion and its past history, retained an identity and tradition that makes this upland area very much 'its own man'. The Borders Region of Scotland (comprised of the districts of Berwickshire, Roxburghshire, Ettrick and Lauderdale, and Tweeddale), and the northern fringes of Northumberland, embrace the land-mass covered in the guide, known as the Borders. The population is in the region of 120,000, the majority of whom reside in a number of small towns and villages, of which only fourteen exceed 1,500. This makes the region the second most thinly populated area in Scotland and certainly the most sparsely inhabited section of England. The average space per head of population in the Borders is one person for every eleven acres, compared with an overall average for Scotland of less than four acres per person.

The fertile farms in the straths of Tweed and Teviot have fostered a fine arable and stock tradition, whilst the surrounding hills have a reputation for breeding and feeding sheep that is second to none, proudly producing named breeds such as The Cheviot and The Border Leicester. Allied with agriculture are the twin spin-offs: quality textiles (the mainstay of the local economy) and food processing. In recent years the industrial base has widened to include such industries as plastics, chemicals, paper production, health care and electronics. All of which has fortunately led to the reversal of the population drift, thus increasing the numbers residing in the area in the last fifteen years. The Borders is also renowned in the field of sport, particularly Rugby Union.

13

This Borderland has a character of its own, manifest not only in the green and rounded hills, the glens and bubbling burns, but also in Border legend, its poems and its music. It's a character that may not be fully understood by a single ascent of Cheviot or a walk in Ettrick Forest, for it is as subtle, yet as certain as the seasons.

The region offers sixty-eight mountains and tops in excess of 2,000 feet, the highest being Broad Law 2,754 feet, with only a smattering of rock climbs and several scrambles on scree or in rocky gullies. The highlights of the area however are the many long and exhilarating ridge walks, even though some may include the notorious peat hags of the upper Cheviots. No matter what your tastes, there are walks in the guide to suit all pedestrians and lovers of the countryside, whatever your abilities and secondary interests.

CLIMATE AND WEATHER PATTERNS

Sunshine	Hours of Bright Sunshine - Daily Average												
Jan	Feb	Mar	Apr	May	Jun	Jul	Aug	Sep	Oct	Nov	Dec	Annual Total
Ettrick Head													
1.3	2.2	2.9	4.5	5.3	5.5	4.6	4.3	3.3	2.5	1.8	1.2	1,198
Lower Tweed													
1.7	2.7	3.7	5.3	6.0	6.6	6.1	5.4	4.3	3.4	2.3	1.6	1,493

The number of hours of sunshine is dependent to a certain extent on the height above sea level, in particular in the vicinity of Cheviot, Hart Fell and Broad Law, whose summits attract precipitation and cloud. Lower Tweeddale, the coastal plain and the more sheltered valleys enjoy up to 50% more sunshine than the hills over 2,000 feet, especially those in the west of the region.

Temperature	Daily Average at Sea Level, in Centigrade	
	Maximum	Minimum
January	6°	0°
July	19.5°	10.5°

The Lapse Rate, a reduction of approximately 3°C for every 1,000 feet increase in height above sea level, allows a simple calculation to be made in relation to the Border walks. Sheltered inland valleys can be colder than the summits during the winter months, as the cold air tends to drain into the valley floors forming frost pockets, whilst the converse is true during the summer.

Visibility

The Borders enjoys very good visibility, situated as it is in a remote area well away from industrial pollution and heavy traffic. Evening and night fogs, should they occur, are formed from water droplets, and as such they invariably clear during the day with the increase in temperature. Sea Haars can be experienced along the Berwickshire coast and may occasionally affect Walk 1, Chapter 2, from April to September.

Wind

Based on readings taken at 1,000 feet, the prevailing wind pattern governing the Border Hills and the Southern Uplands is from the south west; winds blowing from between south and west are at least twice as frequent as from any other point on the compass. 85% of the year the wind speeds are between one and a half to eighteen and a half miles per hour, plus 5% below one mile per hour (graded as calm). Records show that sustained wind speeds never exceed forty-six miles per hour, though occasional gusts may do so. April to October provide the calmest months to walk the Border Hills, with January to March being the coldest and the most windy. During the winter months the uplands can be sterilised by cold north-easters that ride in, from the Arctic or the continental Steppes, on the edge of high pressure systems.

Precipitation

With the prevailing wind pattern from the south-west, and influenced by its journey over the Atlantic Ocean, it is the west of the area that receives most rain. The western bastion of the Tweedsmuir Hills has an average annual fall of 89 inches on Lochcraig Head, 85 inches on Hart Fell, 83 inches on Gameshope Loch and 82 inches on Garelet Dod. The eastern Cheviots (including The Cheviot plateau) by comparison only attract 45 inches, with the lower western tops receiving on average 36 inches, emphasising how dry this area is when compared with the annual deluges of 125 inches occurring in the "fashionable areas" of the Western Highlands and the English Lakes. At the lower levels in Tweeddale and Teviotdale and on the Merse of Berwickshire the annual rainfall ranges from a mere 26 inches to 30 inches.

With showers in mind the Peaks and Troughs for walking in the Borders are:

	Driest in Year	**Wettest in Summer**	**Wettest in Winter**
Cheviots	Mar Apr June	Aug (wettest in year)	Nov Dec Jan
Tweeddale	Mar Apr June	Aug (wettest in year)	Sept Nov Jan
Ettrick Forest	Mar Apr June	Aug	Nov Dec Jan
Moffat Hills	Mar Apr June	Aug	Oct Nov Dec
Manor Hills	Mar Apr June	Aug	Oct Nov Dec

The incidence of summer thunderstorms and hail showers in Scotland as a whole, and the Borders in particular, is low; much less frequent than in parts of England. In Edinburgh, such phenomena appear on average seven times a year, in areas of England on average fifteen to twenty times a year.

In winter snow very rarely impedes the walker, even at heights in excess of 2,000 feet. Any coverings that occur invariably enhance the scene and provide just that little extra challenge.

Average Number of Days Per Month With Snow Lying at 0900 Hours												
Altitude	Jan	Feb	Mar	Apr	May	Jun	Jul	Aug	Sep	Oct	Nov	Dec
1,000 ft	10	9.6	4.7	0.7	0	0	0	0	0	0	1.9	5

Evidence from the weather patterns mentioned above, ie. from records compiled over the last twenty years, would suggest that the month of June provides the Border walker with the brightest and driest days, the best walking temperatures, little or no wind, good visibility and of course long days and short nights. June is closely followed by April, May and July with only a small reduction in either temperature or hours of sunshine, or an acceptable increase in precipitation. All in all a very pleasant climate in which to walk.

FLORA AND FAUNA

Upper Heaths and Moors

This type of terrain dominates the Cheviots, Ettrick Forest, and the Tweedsmuir Hills, where the dry heaths on the steep upper slopes change gradually into peat bogs on the flatter summits and plateaux. Such heathland contains heather (ling), cotton grass (scotsmans heids), and cross leaved heath, all of which grow happily on the wet and acidic peat. Covering the drier slopes bilberry (blaeberry) and bell heather prosper, whilst on well drained summit ridges cloudberry, crowberry and dwarf cornal grow, and on the highest hills the rare alpine foxtail may occasionally be found. Grasses that thrive on the Border hills are mainly matgrass (which turns vast areas of the upper Cheviots white in late summer) and wavy hair grass, whilst in areas of water percolation tussocks of purple moor grass (molinia) make walking difficult. In poor visibility the varying vegetation at higher levels acts as a guide, giving indications of altitude, and warnings of wet and potentially dangerous conditions underfoot.

Sixteen types of birds utilize this habitat to hunt, feed, breed and nest. This area remains one of the last strongholds for such as the peregrine falcon (in the crags), the merlin (hunts over the heather), the hen harrier, dunlin and the golden plover. On the higher craggy hills and gullies, such as Blackhope Glen and the Hen Hole, ravens may be found although in small numbers, whereas carrion crows (the moorland scavenger) are much more common. Few if any animals and reptiles inhabit the summits and the tops, though summer visits may be made by the fox, the blue mountain hare (with its distinctive white coat in winter), and feral goats. "Domestic" sheep are to be found at all levels in the Border hills.

Lower Slopes, Ridges, Cols and Open Moorland

These are blanketed by bent grass, fescues and bracken (becoming a great threat) and, growing in the less acidic soils, patches of red fescue. The colour is provided by blaeberry, catspaw, wild thyme, heath bedstraw, rock rose (food for the rare northern brown argus butterfly [Chapter 2, Walk 1]), and the yellow mountain pansy. Any wet and badly drained areas are clearly indicated by an abundance of rushes and sedge - home to snipe, lizards, slow-worm and frogs;

newts prefer the lower rocks and burn sides. The shy adder, though venomous, is not classed as a highly poisonous snake and can occasionally be seen in the Cheviots basking on a warm rock before slithering off to hide in the bracken.

Sound that is music to the hill walker's ear is provided by two fascinating moorland birds. The distinctive curlew (whaup) with its curved beak and plaintive cry, together with the clown of the fells the peewit (green plover), are both evident in satisfying numbers. Another interesting inhabitant of the heather moors is the short eared owl, who sleeps at night and hunts for voles during the day.

With the encroachment of fast growing pines, larch and spruce, the deer population has greatly increased in recent years, as has the number of stoats, weasels and feral mink, and thankfully woodpeckers.

Lochs and Coastline

Three natural lochs, St Mary's Loch, Loch of the Lowes and Loch Skeen, together with the reservoirs of Talla and Megget, are stocked with trout and inhabited by sea birds. The many burns provide a regular diet for the stately heron and fine sport for anglers, and are home to the ring ouzel and the cheeky little dipper. Three lochans on the northern edge of the Cheviot range also act as staging posts for huge numbers of migratory birds and wintering wildfowl, such as greylag and pinkfooted geese.

The cliffs of St Abb's Head are home to thousands of fulmers, common gulls, razor bills, kittiwakes, shags and puffins, and the cliff-tops a carpet of interesting plants. Further and more specific details can be obtained from the information boards displayed on the walks and from local Tourist Information Centres.

HISTORY

Physical

Time Chart

BC	Significant Events Affecting the Area
60,000,000	Carboniferous Era: Calciferous sandstones as found in the Merse of Berwickshire; volcanoes, eg. the Eildon Hills.
40,000,000	Devonian Era: Red Sandstone and Cheviot Lava.
30,000,000	Silurian Era: A huge earth movement joined the land masses bearing Scotland and England.
12,000 - 10,000	The retreat of the Ice Sheets.
9,000	Invasion by trees and shrubs, moss and lichen and other open-ground vegetation. Tundra conditions.
7,000	Significant rise of the North Sea, with the land bridge to the Continent severed, forming raised beaches.
6,000	Forests of broad-leaved woodland and areas of scrub grew below 2,500 feet, replacing and reducing areas of coniferous forest.
4,000	Elm tree decline, allowing infiltration by ground vegetation into forest clearings.

Human

BC	
6,000 - 3,000	Mesolithic period, penetration along river bank settlements, eg. Rink farm near Galashiels, Kalemouth and Springwood near Kelso.
3,500 - 2,500	Neolithic period, which saw the introduction of a basic form of agriculture.
2,500 - 2,000	The development of a hierarchal society, in which ceremonial objects such as polished stone axes and maces were made.
2,000 - 1,250	Introduction of new types of ceremonial sites such as beaker burials, individual burials in cairns and cists. The erection of stone circles and standing stones, eg. Five Stanes Rig, Nine Stane Rig and Threestone Burn.

1,750	Bronze Age technology introduced into the Borders.
1,500 - 700	An age of open settlements and field cultivations together with hill-top meeting places, eg. the Eildon Hills and the heights surrounding the glen Heatherhope.
700 - 500	Iron Age technology, ring ditch, horseshoe houses with pallisaded settlements, eg. Hownam Rings.
500 - 200	Iron age fortifications, with the development of arable and livestock farming, eg. Glenrathope and The Street.

AD

80 - 105	Roman occupation of the Borders, Flavian's headquarters established at Trimontium, Melrose.
140 - 180	Antonine occupation of the Borders, HQ remained at Trimontium, Melrose.
205 - 212	Severan's Roman campaigns.
400 - 550	With the Roman withdrawl a period of tribal warfare, followed by early Christian crusading by the Celtic communities, eg. The Yarrow Stone.
550 - 1015	Northumbrian political and religious domination of the eastern and central Borders. Monastic settlements established at Jedburgh, Old Melrose, and Coldingham.
1015	Battle of Carham, after which Berwickshire and Teviotdale were incorporated into the kingdom of Scotland.
1128 - 1140	The four great Border Abbeys of Kelso, Melrose, Jedburgh and Dryburgh were completed in the reign of David I of Scotland.
1124 - 1603	Continuous conflict between England and Scotland, during which the Border was trampled underfoot by the armies of both sides. When they had passed through, the Reiver (Fighting Families) on both sides of the Border were at each other's throats. The Reiver had no loyalty save that of a blood relationship.

Reivers strongholds can be seen as Pele Towers at Smailholm, Newark, Dryhope, Kirkhope and, the bloodiest of them all, Hermitage.

1603   The Union of the Crowns, after which there was a hundred year period of pacification before peace and prosperity came to the Borders.

PUBLIC RIGHTS OF WAY

This is a grey and troubled area, and it is not within the remit of this guide to go further than state the four criteria needed to establish and maintain a public right of way.

1. It must have been used by the general public for a continuous period of 20 years.
2. It must have been used as a matter of right.
3. It must connect two public places.
4. It must follow a route more or less defined.

Two publications are recommended, *Public Rights of Way in the Borders Region*, Borders Regional Council, Newtown St Boswells, Melrose, TD6 0SA; and *A Walkers Guide to the Law of Rights of Way in Scotland*, Scottish Rights of Way Society Ltd, 28 Rutland Square, Edinburgh, EH1 2BW.

THE LAW OF TRESPASS DIFFERS IN ENGLAND AND SCOTLAND AND THIS GUIDE IS NOT QUALIFIED TO LEAD THE WALKER THROUGH EITHER MINEFIELD. THE AUTHOR HAS FOUND THAT A SERIOUS AND COURTEOUS ENQUIRY TO THE LANDOWNER, FARMER OR SHEPHERD REGARDING THE FEASIBILITY OF A CERTAIN ROUTE MAKES LIFE SO MUCH EASIER FOR ALL CONCERNED. TO SHOW CONCERN FOR OTHERS' PROPERTY, AS WELL AS THE ENVIRONMENT IS TO SHOW CONCERN FOR THE ENTIRE COUNTRYSIDE.

ACTION

ACCESS AND ACCOMMODATION

Access

Rail Links: Two main lines pass through the Border Hills and the Southern Uplands, stopping at Berwick upon Tweed on the east coast inter-city line, and Carlisle on the west inter-city link between Glasgow and the western areas of England and Wales (Carlisle station is connected to the Central Borders by the Scottish Borders Rail Link bus).

Frequent inter-city services stop at Berwick upon Tweed each day, with several slower stopping trains supplementing this service. Carlisle is served from Glasgow, the west of England, Wales and London. Timetables, tickets and fare details are available from Scotrail and British Rail stations, plus British Rail Travel Agents offices. The telephone numbers of the two stations serving the area are given under Useful Information.

Road Links: By car from the eastern half of England, the A1(M) and M1 roads lead north to Tyneside, and from there the A1 continues north to Berwick upon Tweed. Scenic routes from Newcastle upon Tyne are the A697 road to Wooler and Coldstream (Chapter 1), and the A68 road directly through The Cheviots via Jedburgh to Teviotdale and Tweeddale (Chapters 1 and 2). For southbound travellers four roads lead from Edinburgh direct to the heart of the Borders; the A703 to Peebles (Chapter 4), and the A7 to Selkirk (Chapter 3), the A68 to Melrose and Jedburgh (Chapters 2 and 1), and the A697 to Kelso and Wooler (Chapters 1 and 2).

To reach the Borders from the south-west of England and Wales use the M5 then M6 motorways north to Carlisle, then travel north-east on the A7 Borders scenic route to Langholm, Hawick and Selkirk (Chapter 3). From Glasgow use the A74 to Moffat, then north-east via the A708 road to St Mary's Loch and Selkirk (Chapters 3 and 4).

When a car is used to convey walkers to the start of a walk and parking space is limited, care and consideration should be exercised, to ensure access and passage is not restricted for those who live and work in the area.

Bus Services: Long Distance City Link express bus services from twenty-nine major cities and towns (including four airports) in England and Scotland pass through the eastern Borders, stopping at Galashiels, Selkirk, Hawick and Jedburgh. Western fringes of the area are served with long distance buses from the west of Scotland, England and Wales, calling at Carlisle and Moffat.

Local Services: As in the majority of wild and lonely areas, the Borders is not particularly well served by local bus services. School buses can be used in some areas, as can the Post Bus (remember, many of the remote areas have only one delivery/collection per day). To supplement these services from July to September (inclusive) the Harrier Bus is routed to call at the tourist parts other buses do not reach. The majority of walks in the guide can be reached by a local bus service of one type or another, though not always at times to suit the walker, nor can the return trip be guaranteed. Bus guides are available from Borders Regional Council, bus offices, the Scottish Borders Tourist Board and its tourist information centres, and contacts for bookings etc. are detailed under Useful Information.

Accommodation

The walks are arranged in geographical groups with one base covering several walks, thus reducing the need to be continually hunting for overnight accommodation. A wide and varied selection of accommodation is available in the Borders to suit all tastes and pockets. To assist the walker to find the most convenient place to stay, all walks descriptions list the nearest village/farmhouse providing accommodation.

Accommodation details and booking arrangements can be obtained from tourist information centres and youth hostels, details of which are given under Useful Information.

A GUIDE TO THE GUIDE

Aims

The overall aim is to produce a walks guide that is completely comprehensive, whilst remaining as comfortable and easy to understand as it is to carry. A guide that is graphically explicate and verbally inspiring, thus enabling the walker to traverse the

Borderland with enthusiasm and enjoyment.

The fifty-three walks in the guide have all been walked several times, and a few special favourites many times. The journeys, a fraction of the walks available in the Borders, have been planned to suit all tastes, whether they be that of the committed mountain walker or the leisurely valley stroller.

Lay-Out

The area is divided into four, Chapters 1 to 4, each one self contained and geographically different from its fellows. The mountainous and hilly sections Chapters 1 and 4 obviously contain a high proportion of hill walks, whilst the walks in Chapters 2 and 3 are of a more gentle nature.

Chapter 1 covers twenty walks in The Cheviot range, lonely and isolated and unchanged over the centuries. Chapter 2 describes nine walks in the romantic valleys of the Tweed and its largest tributary the Teviot, whilst Chapter 3 follows in the footsteps of the Border's literary giants of centuries past, with twelve walks in the Ettrick Forest. Chapter 4 embraces with twelve walks the massifs of the Moffat and the Manor Hills.

In Chapter 5 I have included three long distance walks that pass through and finish within the region: (a) the final and the toughest twenty-nine miles of the Pennine Way, (b) the final section of the Alternative Pennine Way and (c) the eastern section of the Southern Upland Way. Also included in this chapter are details of seven Town Trails - walks and strolls of pictorial and historical interest through and round the principal towns of the Borders.

For an easy and quick reference to identify a special interest with a specific walk a special interest table has been compiled, and follows this section.

A Glossary of local names and dialect words relating to the area together with local pronunciations is followed by the Bibliography, and finally lists of addresses for accommodation, transport, various organisations and weather forecasts.

Details and Reasoning in Chapters 1 to 4

Each chapter introduces the area with a portrait of the landscape, and includes a simple map showing the numbered location of each walk within that section. This is then followed by a thumb-nail description of the numbered walks together with details of relevant maps, and, to provide quick and easy reference to such items as Distance, Ascent, Degree of Difficulty and Time for each walk, an Information Table is included. All walks are graded with a Degree of Difficulty classification from one to four (1 being the most gentle walk, 4 the most demanding). The gradings are included in all the Walks Tables, together with a full explanation of the grading, and also in the introduction to the walks description.

Each walk is then described in detail, with an easy-to-read map showing the suggested route, which is then followed by a blow-by-blow account of the way (with six-figure map references and compass bearings if necessary). Instructions to turn Left or Right are accompanied by the instructions, ie. East or West.

The picture is finally completed by Items of Interest Along the Way. For clarity each item is numbered and keyed into the text of the route description, eg. Dryburgh Abbey (1), this leaves the route description uncluttered and easy to follow, whilst allowing the walker to peruse the items of interest at his/her leisure.

The Walks are timed using the established formulae of W.W.Naismith. For each 3 miles (4.8kms) of linear distance allow 1 hour, and should an ascent be made in that distance add 30 minutes to the walking time for each 1,000 feet (305m) of ascent. The resultant times calculated using the Naismith formula have been tempered by my own timings, depending on the type of terrain to be traversed, the weather conditions expected, and the frequency and length of stops. It is not the intention of this guide to map out an assault course.

SPECIAL INTERESTS TABLE

Interest	Chapter	Walk
ANTIQUITY	1	1,3,6,10,11,12,16
	2	1,2,4,5
	3	1,2
	4	8
DROVE ROADS	1	9,10,11,11A,12,15,16,17
	2	6,9
	3	1,3,7
	4	9
FLORA & FAUNA	1	1,2,3,7,9,9A,16,18
	2	1,2,4,5
	3	2,4,8,9
	4	1,2,2A,3,4,9
GEOLOGY	1	1,3,7,9,9A,18
	2	1,4,5
	3	5,8
	4	1,2,2A,3,4,6,8,9,10
HISTORICAL	1	1,2,5,7,10,15,16,18
	2	1,2,3,4,5,6,7,8,9
	3	1,3,4,5,7,10
	4	5,6,8,9,10
LITERARY	2	4
	3	3,4,5,6
	4	10
LOCHS, RIVERS, WATERFALLS	1	2,3,7,14,18
	2	1,2,4,6,9
	3	2,4,5,6,10
	4	1,2,2A,3,5,9
OLD INDUSTRY	1	1,7
	2	5
PHOTOGRAPHY	1	1,3,7,9,9A,11,18

Interest	Chapter	Walk
PHOTOGRAPHY (CONTINUED)	2	1,2,3,4,5,6,7,8,9
	3	1,3,4,5,6,8,9,10
	4	1,2,2A,3,4,5,7,8,9,10
RELIGIOUS	2	1,2,4,5
	3	2,4,6
	4	5,8
SCENIC EXCELLENCE	1	1,2,3,5,7,8,9,9A,10, 11,13,18
	2	1,2,3,4,5,8
	3	1,2,4,5,8,9,9A,9B
	4	1,2,2A,3,4,5,6,7,8,9,10
SCRAMBLING	1	7,9,9A,13
	4	1,2A,3
WALKS-CHALLENGING	1	2,3,7,9,9A,18
	3	8,9
	4	2,2A,3,4,8
WALKS-GENTLE	2	1,2,3,7,8
	3	3,4,10

CLOTHING AND EQUIPMENT

Four simple words ease the vexed question of what to wear and what to take on a walk: "CONDITIONS DETERMINE CLOTHING/ EQUIPMENT". Whether that walk is a leisurely stroll on a balmy summer evening, or a mountain hike on a particularly tempestuous February day, the answer is always the same. Conditions underfoot and overhead will determine the clothing and footwear to wear, and what extra equipment, if any, to take in the sack.

Conditions Underfoot

What to Expect on the Border Hills and the Southern Uplands

The Cheviot Hills, Tweeddale, Ettrick Forest and the Tweedsmuir Hills, at levels below 1,500 feet, are traversed either by farm tracks or grass covered paths, and invariably provide good dry walking. Above 1,500 feet conditions vary a great deal, from narrow dry traces over short and springy grass (as found on Hedgehope and Peel Fell), to trenches of glutinous peat (the summit plateau of Cheviot). Areas of wet peat do give the observant walker warning signals. Should a summit or ridge exhibit *legs* of heather running down from the top (similar to a rich brandy sauce flowing over a Christmas pudding), beware, there are peat hags and wet conditions on the apex. Avoid patches of bright green moss such as sphagnum or featherbed moss, they invariably grow over wet-holes. Cotton grass and rushes also signal water underfoot and should be given a wide berth if possible. Bilberry, bents and molinia grass on the other hand signal dry paths, so choose your footwear accordingly.

Lightweight boots or well soled trainers for the lower levels, middleweight leather boots for the higher levels and leather rigid soled boots for scrambling and rock traverses are recommended. Footwear chosen wisely will shorten the journey, take the wrong option and the walk could be a disaster. The question of how many socks to wear is a matter of personal choice, the guideline, be comfortable.

Conditions Overhead

What to expect on the Border Hills and the Southern Uplands

The area, being situated in the eastern half of the country, is not prone to excess precipitation as is experienced in the vicinity of Fort William or the English Lakes. Nor does it suffer from severe cold due to high altitude, as the hills rarely exceed 2,500 feet, though occasionally when the air stream is from the north-east the winds are known locally as *thin*. Hours of sunshine are also above the national average, but because of the latitude temperatures never become unbearable. Choose clothes to keep you warm and dry in winter, and in summer choose loose fitting garments made of natural fibres that breathe freely, plus a hat to protect against the sun's rays, and carry a large filled water bottle.

Two physical factors are of prime importance to the hill walker, temperature and moisture. If both are in balance and agreeable to the pedestrian then the walk will be a pleasure. Should that not be so, and the hiker is ill-prepared and ill-equipped, he/she is unwisely exposing him/her self to the twin risks of hypothermia and dehydration/heat exhaustion. Hypothermia can strike if the temperature of the body core drops below 98.4°F in continuous cold and wet conditions. Dehydration or heat exhaustion can be induced by exposing the body, and in particular the head, to excess heat, coupled with an inadequate liquid intake.

Wind is a major factor in deciding what to wear and can have a marked effect in both winter and summer on the Border Hills. In winter there is always the threat of a chilling north-easter, therefore the wind chill factor must always be considered. An increase of 10 miles per hour in wind speed can reduce the temperature from 18°C to 7°C, or in colder conditions from 10°C to -13°C. Also bear in mind the lapse rate. The higher the climb the lower the temperature, for every 1,000 feet ascended there is a reduction of approximately 3°C.

Experienced and committed pedestrians are sure to carry their favourite talisman to protect them from the evil eye of the elements. For those not yet into the mystique of what's in the walker's sack (which should be lined with a plastic bin-liner), let me list the essentials that are needed for high and low level walks in the Borders.

High Level

A windproof and waterproof anorak/cagoule, waterproof overtrousers or gaiters, a woolly hat (cotton in the summer), woollen gloves/mitts, and a survival bag. High energy food (the average high level walk in this guide will burn up 1,500 calories above the normal metabolic rate), with a hot drink in winter/large water filled bottle in summer. Emergency rations such as dried fruit, chocolate, glucose tablets/Kendal mint cake or Christmas cake (if in season), should be included for all high and long walks.

Low Level

Walking in summer at the lower levels, particularly in the sheltered valleys, can induce heat exhaustion/dehydration if the walker is unprotected and exposed for long periods. A lightweight cotton hat with a floppy brim, and a full water bottle, will provide all the protection needed. The debate of shorts versus long trousers generates too much heat to offer an opinion, suffice it to say some walkers prefer cool scratched legs, whilst others prefer protected legs, albeit hot and white.

This guidebook should also be carried at all times.

SAFETY

Whilst all the walks in the guide are designed primarily for the walkers pleasure, safety in the great outdoors is something we must all be aware of. A careless step into a rabbit scrape or on a loose stone could break a bone or tear a tendon, causing a major problem for the solitary walker. As many of the walks may be completed in total solitude it is prudent to be familiar with emergency procedures, and the equipment needed to minimise discomfort and aid rescue in the unlikely event of an accident occurring.

Equipment

1. First-aid kit, including sterile dressings, lint/zinc tape, antiseptic cream, crepe/elasticated bandages (tubi-grip), scissors/knife, and medication (including salt tablets, pain killers etc.). The medication must only be for personal use, it is unwise and risky to administer medication to another unless medically qualified.

2. A basic knowledge of first-aid should be carried in the head or in the sack.

3. A knife, torch (with a spare bulb and batteries), whistle, spare laces (double up as bindings), emergency food and water, survival bag, compass and map, paper and pen/pencil.

Action

1. Prevention is always better than cure, as advocated by two pedestrian giants of the past, Edward Whymper and A.Wainwright, who both suggested "a walk or even a life could be ruined by careless placement of the feet".

2. Solitude in the hills is to be prized and is much sought after, but from the safety angle solo walks are to be avoided, the ideal number being five walkers of a like mind and similar ability. Such perfection is rarely possible, therefore to reduce the risks on the hills observe a few simple guidelines and use that under-employed asset, common sense.

3. Always inform someone of your route and estimated time of return (ETR). If that is not possible leave your route plan with details, ie. destination, number in the party, colour of the

garments and the ETR, in a visible position in the car. One school of thought thinks this is an invitation to the car thief, cars however can be replaced when lost, human life cannot.

4. Should you have the misfortune to be immobilised and require help use the International rescue call - six long blasts on a whistle, or flashes with a torch and repeat at one minute intervals. The reply is three short blasts at minute intervals. Should you be without whistle or torch, SHOUT using the same code. When waiting for help, use the terrain to gain protection from the elements. Shelter from wind and rain/snow, or the sun in summer, and utilise spare clothing and the survival bag (feet pointing to the wind), to maintain body temperature.

5. Should an accident occur when with a companion, write your position on paper (a six figure map reference - "Eastings" first, ie. the immediate vertical grid line to the left of your position, then the number of tenths from the grid line to your position, then "Northings" repeating the procedure using the horizontal grid line below the position - as instructed on the legend of the OS map). Include the name, injury and time sustained, general health, age and clothing, and dispatch the able-bodied party to the nearest telephone, (farmhouse etc, or public telephone as shown on the OS map). On reaching the telephone dial 999 (police), who on receiving full details of the accident, will call out the local mountain rescue team and co-ordinate the rescue operation. When the mountain rescue team is requested, the victim MUST STAY PUT until help arrives.

Two mountain rescue teams cover the Borders, the Cheviot Mountain Rescue (based at Kelso and Yetholm), and the Tweed Valley Mountain Rescue (based at Selkirk). The principal Borders hospital is the Borders General, Huntlyburn, Melrose.

COUNTRY CODE

Respect the countryside and all that lives and grows therein, and endeavour to leave it in a better state than you found it. Should these aims be achieved, not only will it give you the walker pleasure, but also the Countryside Commission for Scotland whose Country Code states:

1. Guard against all risk of fire.
2. Fasten all gates.

3. Keep all dogs under complete control. Do not take dogs on the open fell during lambing time.
4. Use stiles and gates to cross fences, stone dykes etc.
5. Keep to public rights of way, bridlepaths and footpaths, and do not step onto crops on farmland.
6. Leave livestock, crops and farm machinery alone, no matter how appealing or interesting they may look.
7. If you can carry a full crisp packet to the summit of a mountain, you can carry the empty packet back. Take your litter home.
8. Do not pollute any water supplies.
9. Do not disturb or damage wildlife, plants or trees.
10. Respect others' property and privacy, treat it as you would have others treat yours.
11. Prejudices should be left at home.

Grouse Rearing and Shooting. Respect the property of those who live and work on the moors. The grouse shooting season runs from August 12th to December 10th.

Bulls and Adders are also best avoided. The adder (60cm in length, brown with a dark zig-zag on the back) is more concerned in avoiding contact with humans. Bulls are somewhat larger and have no such inhibitions.

CONVERSION TABLE AND MAPS LEGEND

Conversion Table			
FEET (ft)	METRES (m)	MILES	KILOMETRES (km)
1,000	304.80	1	1.609
1,250	381.00	2	3.219
1,500	457.20	3	4.828
1,750	533.40	4	6.437
2,000	609.60	5	8.047
2,250	685.80	6	9.656
2,500	762.00	7	11.265
2,750	838.20	8	12.875
3,000	914.40	9	14.484
		10	16.039
		15	24.086
		20	32.187

Linhope Spout (Walk 1.3).
Entire circuit of Walk 1.6, Halterburn Valley.

The Shearers and Craik Moor (Walk 1.11)
Heatherhope Valley (Walk 1.14)

MAPS LEGEND

✕	START OF WALK
·—·—·—·—·	BOUNDARY NATIONAL/ REGIONAL
▭ ⬤	VILLAGE OR TOWNSHIP
▭	FARM OR HOUSE
≋	ROAD SUITABLE FOR MOTORISED VEHICLE
·—→——→·	ROUTE/FOOTPATH
⊤⊤⊤⌢	DISMANTLED RAILWAY
⬯	LOCH/RESERVOIR
⌒⌒	RIVER
∿∿∿	BURN/STREAM
≍	BRIDGE
▲	SUMMIT OF MOUNTAIN/HILL
!	HIGH EXPOSURE, CRAG, SCREE OR GORGE
♙	CAIRN
○	ANCIENT SETTLEMENT/FORT
❘	STANDING STONE
✚	ABBEY/CHURCH/MONASTERY
✜	CASTLE/PELE TOWER
△	TOWER
●	MONUMENT
♧♧ ⇈	FOREST/PLANTATION
	(BROAD LEAVED/CONIFERS)

33

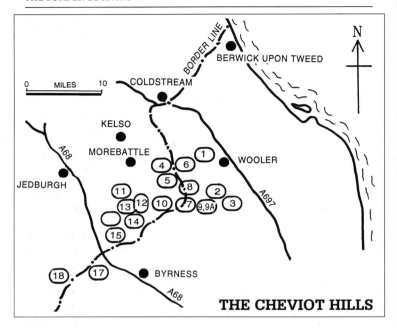

THE CHEVIOT HILLS

Chapter 1: The Cheviot Hills

THE AREA

Endless ridges straddle the eastern and central border of England and Scotland, in a tangle of green and rounded summits split asunder by steep sided, sinuous valleys. Windswept grasses continually ebb and flow over these upland fells, with the plaintive cries of the whaup and the peewit, together with the bleating of sheep, more often heard than the human voice. The hills and mountains of the Cheviots could never be likened unto the oft exhaulted giants of the Western Highlands, or the winsome English Lakes, yet they have an appealing romanticism, these lonely and now peaceful hills.

The principal summits are clustered in the east, as supplicants to the massif of The Cheviot 2,676 feet (after whom the range is named), and with the exception of Windy Gyle, Auchope Cairn and The Schil (which straddle the Border ridge), they all rise in England. Of these Hedgehope, Cairn Hill, Comb Fell, Bloody Bush Edge, and Cushat Law all top 2,000 feet. At the western extremity of the range the principal hills of Peel Fell and Carter Fell also have a foot on each side of the Border. By the very nature of the Cheviot terrain it is possible for the hill walker to traverse the tops without any great loss of height or energy, whilst still maintaining a steady pace.

Pathways, trails and directional markers are sparse, and in places non-existent (with the exception of the Pennine Way, some Roman roads and the occasional drove road). Although the majority of walks are over paths and trails that ease the walker's progress, there are isolated locations where "traffic" is heavy. The summit plateau of Cheviot and sections of the Pennine Way can degenerate in adverse weather, into a mire that is well nigh impassable. Exposed rock in the Cheviots is a shy bird, rarely revealing itself in any quantity, making these hills an unhappy hunting ground for the rock climber, and an area with only an occasional pitch for the scrambler, (Walks 7, 9, 9A, 13, and 18 include scrambles).

The majority of "walk-ins" are from the Scottish side, where the approaches are not hindered by the serried ranks of conifers in the forests of Kielder and Redesdale. Nor are the Scottish foothills restricted by the activities of a very active MOD as at Redesdale, whose high-powered missiles "crump" daily into the English side of the range.

Few if any roads, apart from the A68 at Carter Bar, cross the main ridge north to south, nor is there a continuous road that encircles the Cheviots, which results in miles of unpopulated uplands. Apart from occasional isolated hill farms scattered thinly over the area the only habitation is in a few villages and hamlets on the extremities of the range. Small towns such as Wooler, Kelso and Jedburgh are situated in the surrounding valleys, some ten miles from the higher ground. This scattered and sparse population, whilst enhancing the isolation factor so beloved by walkers, can create a problem for the adventurer who lacks transport. Local bus services, or the Post Bus, can and do assist in such cases.

THE WALKS

Maps recommended: OS 1:50,000 LANDRANGER, Sheets 74 and 80.

In this chapter are eighteen walks, two of which include a variation of the main walk, making an overall total of twenty. Walk 1 starts in the picturesque College Valley and ascends the eastern Cheviots, a fine introduction to the outlyers of "Muckle Cheviot". Walk 2 surmounts Cheviot, the highest mountain in the range, by a well-worn path that offers the energetic fine views of the Border Hills and the Tweed Valley. Walk 3 climbs the second highest mountain in Northumbria, includes the finest waterfall in the Cheviots, and traverses moorland and forest with only the birds and animals for company.

A change of start brings Walk 4 to Scotland, where the Halterburn Valley winds through the gentle northern foothills, by the high road and the low road. The Halterburn Horseshoe describes Walk 5 perfectly, a ridge walk of high quality encircling the entire valley. Walk 6 follows a Reivers way into England , passing two lonely Border hill farms, several ancient settlements, a burial cairn or two, and several thousand sheep.

Remaining in Scotland, the next five walks have their Alpha and Omega at the historic farm of Cocklawfoot, deep in the Bowmont Valley. Walk 7 is rich in scenery, wildlife, history, legend and personal reward, though a deal of effort is needed to scramble up the Hen Hole, and negotiate the corrie to Auchope Cairn. Walk 8 has a long but pleasant walk-in to The Schil, at 1985 feet the most spectacular non-mountain in the Cheviots. Walk 9 and Walk 9A will demand effort and experience from the walker, and involves rock scrambling, bog-hopping and use of map and compass. The ability to identify World War II aircraft will also add interest. Walk 10 by comparison is a much easier more sedate walk, over the historic and scenic path to the summit of Windy Gyle, a fine walk on a summer's evening, a gem on a crisp winter's day with a few inches of fresh snow underfoot.

Further west along the Border ridge to the tiny hamlet of Hownam Walk 11 and Walk 11A both follow the trails of our Iron Age ancestors, the Legions of Rome and the cattle drovers, the ascent of Hownam Law brings the walker to the very edge of the northern Cheviots. Secluded Greenhill is the start of Walk 12, a fine ridge and valley walk into the heart of a complex of Iron Age settlements; good paths and tracks add bounce to the step. Walk 13 penetrates deeper into the heart of the Cheviots, via the deserted Yett Valley, before ascending the summit of Callaw Cairn. The black waters of Heatherhope start Walk 14, bound for The Street, the Border Ridge and Callaw Cairn to the mysterious Church Hope Hill. Tow Ford on the upper reaches of Kale Water is the start and finish of Walk 15, which ventures into England via Dere Street to visit a Roman Encampment at Chew Green. Walk 16 marches north to the edge of the high ground, to return along another section of

Dere Street, past the ancient stone circle of "Five Stanes" to finish at the Roman marching camp of Pennymuir. The Border crossing of Carter Bar, starts Walk 17 over Carter Fell to visit five old drift mines. Walk 18 passes through the Border Forest Park, before breaking out across a wild and invigorating fell to the Kielder Stane, at 1,500 tons the largest and most remote "post office" on the Border.

INFORMATION TABLE

WALK	DISTANCE/ MILES	ASCENT	DEGREE OF DIFFICULTY*	TIME/ HOURS
1	11	1,463ft	3	6
2	8	2,000ft	4	5¹/₂/6
3	13	2,198ft	4	7¹/₂
4	5	984ft	2	3¹/₂
5	8¹/₂	1,804ft	2	6
6	8	1,070ft	2	4
7	8	2,414ft	4	6
8	7	1,263ft	2	4¹/₂
9	15	2,674ft	4+	8¹/₂
9A	11¹/₂	2,006ft	4	7¹/₂
10	7	1,276ft	2	4
11	10¹/₂	2,309ft	3	6/7
11A	7	1,798ft	2	4¹/₂
12	7	915ft	2	4
13	7¹/₂	1,155ft	2	4¹/₂
14	8	1,171ft	2	5
15	10	1,250ft	2	6¹/₂
16	10	722ft	2	5
17	7	561ft	2	4
18	12	1,385ft	3	7

*Degree of Difficulty
1 - Good path, moderate ascent, no navigational problems.
2 - Distinct path, steeper ascents, longer walk.
3 - Paths rough in places, ascent 2,000ft, exposed in places.
4 - Few paths, ascent 2,400ft plus, exposed, compass needed.

WALK 1. HETHPOOL - YEAVERING BELL - TOM TALLONS CRAG - NEWTON TORS - HETHPOOL

A fine introduction to the Cheviot Range, involving 11 miles of fell walking with 1,463 feet of stimulating ascent. Classed as grade 3, the circuit should be completed in 6 hours. High on views and historical interest. In low visibility or adverse weather conditions a compass and map are necessary.

A narrow road (signposted Hethpool 1½ miles) branches south-west from the B6351 at Westnewton, to the historic house of Hethpool (1). Cars are not allowed beyond Hethpool cottages without a permit, and parking is limited to the grass verges.

Start the walk at the corner opposite the cottages, a few paces ahead on the left (signposted Old Yeavering) pass through a gate onto the farm track leading to a wooden bridge across the College Burn. Here the way forks left, and ascends to a coniferous plantation. Continue through the trees on a wide but wet track. On clearing the

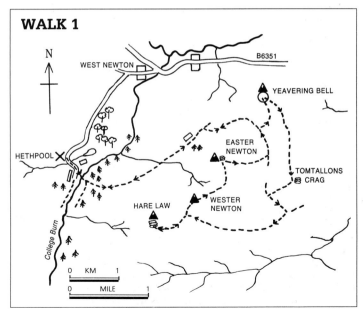

WALK 1

trees follow the path east then north-east via the waymarks to the open fell. High above to the south the twin peaks of Newton Tors (2) smile invitingly down, and ahead 2 miles to the north-east, the distinctive cone of Yeavering Bell (3) 1,182 feet, beckons. Continue on the gently rising track past Torleehouse Farm (4), to the second gate east of the steading. At the gate turn sharp right to follow the wall and a steeply rising farm track to the next gate by a stile. Cross the wall via the stile to continue south; Yeavering Bell is now across the gully to the left. At the next gate, do not pass through but turn left to follow the fence on a faint sheep trace through the bracken. After crossing the first burn select one of many sheep tracks to the summit of Yeavering Bell, passing a sheep stell and a broken wall. The summit carries a large Iron Age fort encircled with stone fortifications, making the final few yards rather difficult; the reward is a complete circle of outstanding views.

Leave the summit on its south side and descend to a small gate in the fence below, a bearing of 160°, ie. east of south leads for 1 mile to the rocky outcrop of Tom Tallons Crag (5) 1,153 feet. From the Crag the grassy path is rejoined 300 yards to the west, follow it south to the gate in the stone dyke. Turn right, ie. west, and follow the wall to another gate where a jeep track swings right leading to the col below Newton Tors, passing Wackerage cairn.

At the col the path joins a wide grassy track which is followed left, ie. south, towards the formidable bulk of The Cheviot, only to swing north to the final col dividing Newton Tors 1,759 feet and Hare Law 1,703 feet. At this point the large pointed cairn on Hare Law is clearly visible to the left. Leave the track to join the stone dyke leading west to the summit of Hare Law, where the summit cairn provides a fine grandstand from which to gaze upon the north face of Cheviot, and admire the elegant sweep of the College Valley far below. Return via the stone dyke to the jeep track and walk north to the summit of Newton Tors, with its rocks and cairn on the north-east shoulder. Another superb eyrie from which to appreciate the surrounding hills and the Northumberland coastline.

Descend from the outcrop, north-north-east past Easter Tor, to join the farm track north to Torleehouse Farm. This is the waymarked pathway that was ascended on the outward journey, and should be followed south-west to the wooden bridge over the College Burn and Hethpool House. A pleasant end to this scenic introduction to the Cheviot Hills. *Accommodation and refreshments are available at Wooler and local B&Bs.*

Items of Interest Along the Way

(1) HETHPOOL. The "pool under Great Hetha", a hill to the south-west. The present house was built in 1919, on the site of the 1685 building. In the garden are the remains of a Pele tower circa 1415, described in a report of 1541 as " a lytle stone house of pyle which ys a greate releyffe to the tennants thereof".

Admiral Lord Collingwood, second in command at the battle of Trafalgar, lived for many years at Hethpool, and always carried a pocketful of acorns for planting, oak trees for future "men of war". Today many of the resultant oaks can be seen in the oak wood at Hethpool Bell.

(2) NEWTON TORS. This attractive hill is a challenge and a pleasure to behold. A northern outlier of Cheviot and flanking the eastern side of the College Valley it was formed some 400 million years ago from laval outpourings from the Cheviot volcanoes. The two tops, Newton Tors and Hare Law, are both capped with distinct and handsome cairns.

(3) YEAVERING BELL. The conical hill, on which stood the largest Iron Age hill fort in Northumbria. Prominent elliptical earthworks and ditches together with the foundations of horseshoe shaped dwellings can still be seen.

(4) TORLEEHOUSE. Once known as "Tarleazes", so called because the land is a clearing on a hill.

(5) TOM TALLONS CRAG. Contrary to popular belief this is not the burial place of Tom Tallon. The name is derived from the Celtic tomen or tal (a forehead or promontory) and llan (enclosure); although many years ago a cairn covering a cist stood close by the crag.

WALK 2. LANGLEEFORD - SCALD HILL - THE CHEVIOT - CAIRN HILL - HARTHOPE BURN - HARTHOPE LINN - LANGLEEFORD

No walking guide covering the Borders would be complete without at least one pilgrimage to the summit of Great Cheviot, at 2,676 feet the highest mountain in the Cheviot Hills. The circular walk of 8 miles includes a total ascent of 2,000 feet, with a journey time of 5¹/₂/6 hours (7 hours in poor conditions) and a degree of difficulty grading of 4. Good boots and mountain clothing are essential, as are a compass and map. Whatever the weather this walk will be a challenge, perhaps best described as beauty and the beast.

At the south end of the main street in Wooler turn right, signposted Middleton Hall and Harthope Valley, to travel 4¹/₂ miles south-west to Langleeford. Parking is possible on the grass verges prior to Langleeford before the small bridge that marks journey's end for unauthorised vehicles; maps and walks details are displayed courtesy of the Northumberland National Park.

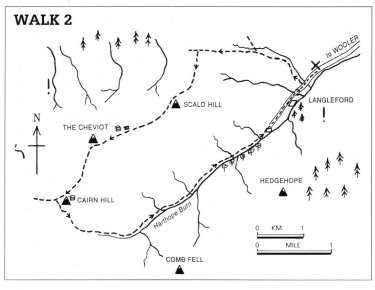

WALK 2

Cheviot summit

Start at the road to travel south west for 200 yards towards Langleeford (1), to the signpost indicating "Scald Hill 1³/₄ miles, The Cheviot 3¹/₂ miles". A good path rises rapidly through bracken and acres of bonny blooming heather, to the flat and grassy summit of Scald Hill 1,797 feet. Leave Scald Hill via a stile to join a conspicuous path alongside the fence running south-south-west, across a wet and peaty saddle, later to rise steeply as a blackened and badly eroded wound in the east side of Cheviot. The final assault of 500 feet is made easier if the northern side of the fence with heather, bilberries and short grass underfoot is used. Once the plateau rim is reached thirteen untidy granite cairns waymark the path to a large shelter cairn, topped by a prominent wooden post on the 2,600 foot contour. Seventy yards west of the shelter cairn stands a smaller cairn with a leaning post, from where the trig point on Cheviot's summit can be seen due west close to the faithful fence.

At this point the path is good underfoot, and on a fine and clear day you will surely consider this to be the finest of walks. In low cloud with squally rain pulsing in on a fractious wind, you may question your sanity; for to the uninitiated the summit of Cheviot (2) 2,676 feet, may prove to be somewhat of a shock, five square miles of featureless and seemingly endless peat hags. In such conditions it would be prudent to retrace your steps.

The route to the trig point follows no specific path, and is very much a matter of personal preference, but always keep the fence to the left and no further away than 100 yards. The summit should be reached within 3 hours from the start, and from its peaty surrounds Cairn Hill 2,545 feet (a small mound with an accompanying cairn) is clearly visible to the south-west. The walk to Cairn Hill is best accomplished by keeping well to the right of the fence and using sheep tracks if possible (sheep do not like getting their feet wet any more than we do). Avoid at all costs the left, ie. south side of the fence, where two menacing ponds await the unwary. Leave Cairn Hill and the guiding fence by the stile close to the cairn, descending due south for 500 yards, across a wilderness of heather and matgrass, then swing south-east towards the bare cleft of red earth that cradles the infant Harthope Burn.

Once the burn is met follow it eastwards, with the running water on the right. As the burn gathers strength the path becomes more obvious, and the walk in the narrow valley between Cheviot and Hedgehope assumes a mantle of tranquillity. Small and stunted silver birch cling precariously to the steep banks, shortly to be joined by alder and rowan, as the noise of gushing water assails the ears. Harthope Linn (3), with its main cascade plunging through the narrowest of gorges is extremely compelling, but take care when hunting for that extra special "close-up".

From the Linn it is but a short 2 miles to Langleeford via the farm steading of Langleeford Hope, along a pleasant farm road and over more stiles, to the tree lined whitewashed buildings of Langleeford the end of an adventure. *Wooler provides a wide variation of accommodation and refreshment.*

Items of Interest Along the Way

(1) LANGLEEFORD. Surrounded by oak, beech, rowan, hazel, ash, and silver birch, Langleeford was first referred to in 1552, in connection with night watches for marauding reivers from Scotland. In 1791 that most romantic of Border walkers, Sir Walter Scott, took a holiday at the farmhouse, enjoying the fishing and the walking, and was particularly taken with the pretty milkmaid who brought him goats milk every morning.

(2) THE CHEVIOT. Standing at 2,676 feet, The Cheviot (locally called Cheviot), is the highest mountain in the Cheviot range. The area was fashioned some 400 million years ago by intense volcanic activity, followed by lava flows, a process that was to continue for many millenium. More recently in 1728, Daniel Defoe ascended Cheviot on horseback, and was "much afraid" he would find the summit a "knife edged ridge". His guides, local boys from Wooler, were greatly amused at this, assuring him "an army could stand upon the top". The first Ordnance Survey was carried out in the early 1800s by the military, and a trig point placed on Cheviot's summit. No less than two trig points have since disappeared into the peat. The present monolith is mounted on a concrete plinth, supported on an 11 foot pile. Many experienced "Cheviotiers" are under no illusions that the present trig point is in the process of joining its predecessors.

(3) HARTHOPE BURN AND HARTHOPE LINN. The source of the burn rises on the south-west flank of Cheviot and tumbles down the Harthope Valley to Langleeford and beyond. A geological fault caused the steep-sided valley to be formed, later glaciers from Cheviot scoured and shaped it into the picturesque valley we know today. Several small waterfalls of amber peat laden water tumble merrily down the upper reaches, the largest and most spectacular being Harthope Linn with a cascade of 25 feet, 2 miles upstream from Langleeford.

WALK 3. LANGLEEFORD - HARTHOPE CRAGS - HEDGEHOPE - LINHOPE SPOUT - LINHOPE - THREESTONEBURN HOUSE - LANGLEE CRAGS - LANGLEEFORD

A challenging and rewarding circular walk of 13 miles, ascending 2,198 feet over a variety of paths, some firm and waymarked others over rough moorland. Linhope Spout provides an idyllic halfway house on this high level walk. Graded with a degree of difficulty of 3, the journey should take 7¹/₂ hours. In adverse weather or poor visibility, compass and map skills are essential, as are boots and warm clothing.

Five miles south-west of Wooler, deep in the Harthope Valley, stands the farm of Langleeford. Car parking is available on the grass verges some 400 yards north-east of the farm, close by the Northumberland National Park advisory signs and maps (with good advice for all).

Start the walk at the road bridge, where a signpost directs the walker 2¹/₂ miles south-west to the conical summit of Hedgehope Hill (1) 2,348 feet. Harthope Burn is crossed by footbridge, from where a waymarked path leads south over three stiles to the open fell, to the distinct outcrops of Housey Crags (2) and Lang Crags (2). Leave Lang Crag at its south-west corner via the stile, following the distinct path for 1 mile south-west, across the wet wastes of Kelpie Strand.

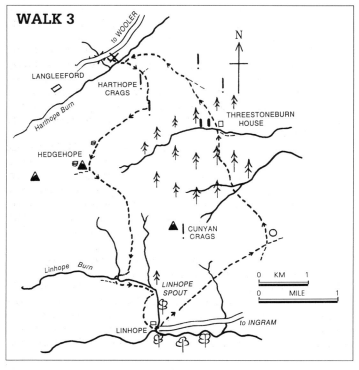

A change in the vegetation underfoot clearly signals the ascent of Hedgehope. Rushes, bright green moss and cotton grass give way to bents, bilberries and matgrass, as the faint waymarked path climbs steeply. First north-west then west to the remains of an old fence, visible on the immediate skyline. At the broken fence turn south, ie. left, and climb steadily past a cairn to the summit of Hedgehope (1), topped by a large dilapidated shelter cairn.

Leave the summit through a gateway on the south side to descend sharply on a well-worn track for 2 miles. The route wends south-east and south between Het Burn and Dunsmoor Burn to a farm road by Linhope Burn. On crossing the burn turn left onto a grassy track, to the spectacular waterfall of Linhope Spout (3). This idyllic and sheltered spot provides an ideal picnic area; it is also greatly favoured by the more adventurous motorist.

A good pathway leads south from Linhope Spout for $^1/_2$ mile to Linhope House. Skirt around the house and cross Linhope Burn to the "permissive" path, signposted "Threestoneburn House, $3^1/_2$ miles". Join the path below the prominent earthworks, and walk $1^3/_4$ miles in a north-easterly direction passing a ruined village close by the "crossroads'. Turn north-north-west, ie. left to pass below Cunyan Crags (2), rising majestically on the eastern shoulder of Dunmoor Hill 1,860 feet. The path continues north-north-west to the forest, which is entered through a gate.

Navigation is not easy in this forest. A bearing of 340° magnetic (varying plus or minus 5°) leads after 1 mile to a clearing 250 yards south of Threestoneburn House. Continue north to the house, which is avoided by crossing a footbridge (waymarked with a blue arrow) west of the house. The arrow and the path directs the walker to a forest gate and stile several hundred yards ahead. Threestoneburn Stone Circle (4) is 400 yards west of the house on the north side of the burn.

The short northern section of the forest is traversed by a faint path through a narrow ride immediately north of the stile and gate. Fifteen minutes of coarse forest walking will clear the trees.

A bearing of 340° magnetic leads past a metal shed and a circle of upright wooden poles. The grass track is now distinct as it travels first north, then north-west between the spectacular rocky outcrops of Middleton Crags (2) and Langlee Crags (2). Once the ridge ahead is breasted descend north-north-west to Harthope Valley and Langleeford. *Wooler provides food and accommodation.*

Items of Interest Along the Way

(1) HEDGEHOPE HILL 2,343 feet. Meaning "head of the valleys", this mountain is the second highest peak in the Cheviot range. Because of its distinctive conical shape, and its position on the south-east corner of the range, it appears as one of the most distinctive mountains in the Cheviots. From the summit on a clear day fine views unfold of the Northumbrian coastal plain, the island of Lindisfarne, the northern Pennines to Cross Fell and the peaks of the northern Lakes.

(2) HOUSEY CRAGS, LANG CRAGS, CUNYAN CRAGS, MIDDLETON CRAGS AND LANGLEE CRAGS. Four hundred million years ago a great mass of molten rock welled up beneath the volcanoes of Cheviot and Hedgehope, eventually cooling to form granite. When this molten mass came into contact with volcanic larva its intense heat changed it chemically into a somewhat different and harder rock. Today we have a circle of this changed rock, 'The Metamorphic Aureole', around Cheviot and Hedgehope. Natural weathering has worn away the softer rock, leaving the harder rocks exposed as visible outcrops. Later the Ice Age fashioned the crags by shearing and streamlining the rocks with the directional movement of the ice, in this case north and south.

(3) LINHOPE SPOUT. The most spectacular of all the Cheviot waterfalls, plunging 56 feet into a deep rock pool, 7 feet across and 15 feet deep. When Linhope Burn is in full spate the cascade is an awesome sight as it thunders into the pool below and hurries on between overhanging birches.

(4) THREESTONEBURN STONE CIRCLE. The stones were arranged elliptically, with 13 shafts, the tallest standing over 5 feet. Sadly today only 5 standing stones remain. It has long puzzled the author as to why the burn should be named so. With 13 stones originally in the circle it would have been logical to name it "Thirteenstoneburn". Could it be that "three" has through time become a mispronunciation of "thirteen"?

WALK 4. HALTERBURN VALLEY - PENNINE WAY - BORDER
FENCE - WHITE LAW - OLD HALTERBURN - BURNHEAD -
HALTERBURN VALLEY

*A gentle introduction to the foothills of the Cheviots, this grade 2 walk of
5 miles includes a section of the Pennine Way (with fine views of the higher
Cheviots), coupled with a picturesque walk in the Halterburn Valley. Good
paths and an easy ascent of 984 feet make this 3½ hour journey a pleasure.*

The walk begins and ends at GR 840277, though it can begin and
end in Kirk Yetholm (1), adding a further 2 miles. At the northern
end of Halterburn Valley a cattle grid signals the starting point
(limited car parking on the verges of the farm track to the left). From
the start make for the stream (Halter Burn), which is easily forded
in summer, not so easy in winter. With a stone dyke on the left for
200 yards, follow the track eastward contouring the hillside as far as
the sheep pens and a Pennine Way marker post. Ascend east-south-
east with the grassy track until the Border Fence (2) is reached. The
boundary between Scotland and England is marked by a dry stone
dyke, which changes later to a wire and post fence.

At the gate on the Border Fence another Pennine Way signpost
directs the walker due south to the col below the summit of White

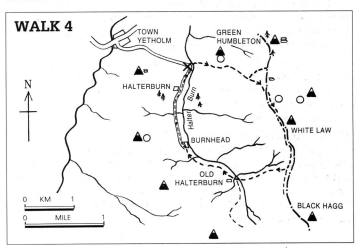

Law (3) 1,407 feet. As this is a wet and boggy path, it is advisable to pass through the gate into England, and follow one of the many dry sheep tracks parallel to the wall and rising to the col $^1/_2$ mile south. This col with its T junction of stone dykes and stile is clearly visible on the skyline. At the T junction turn left and ascend for 150 yards to the summit of White Law 1,407 feet, the highest point of the walk and a fine vantage point.

A few yards beyond the peak of White Law, the Border Fence (now a wire and post fence) turns right, ie. south, and descends sharply to the saddle 300 feet below. Here a small gate in the fence marks the point where the route leaves the Pennine Way (4), by turning right, ie. west, onto a descending track, through the bracken clad hillside of Steer Rig to the ruin of Old Halterburn in the valley below.

Leave the sad ruins of Old Halterburn to the squabbling rooks, and take the farm track north along the valley floor to the working farm of Burnhead. From Burnhead for $1^1/_2$ miles it is a pleasant stroll (5) to the starting cattle grid allowing the walker time to pause and "smell the roses".

Items of Interest Along the Way

(1) KIRK YETHOLM. This small village, so close to the English border, was at one time the rallying point for the Scottish Border gypsies, providing a convenient spring-board from which to nip over into England in times of strife. A far cry from 1540 when the Gypsy King John Faa signed a treaty with James V of Scotland, in which he was described as "Our lovit Johnne Faa, Lord and Earl of littl Egypt". The last king, Charles Blyth Faa (whose coronation coach was drawn by six donkeys), died in 1802, was succeeded by a Gypsy Queen.

(2) THE BORDER FENCE. The first written evidence of the actual position of the eastern Border was in AD 1173, when reference was made to the river Tweed as the Border. In 1222 a joint boundary commission met to define the Border but the task proved to be too much, so only a small section was agreed upon. Further work between 1542 and 1604 achieved little. The Border as we know it today seems to have been born between 1604 and 1648, after the "Union of the Crowns" in 1603. Today the present Border Fence

remains an extremely useful navigational aid, and many have good reason to be grateful for its presence on these bleak and lonely hills (see Chapter 1, Walk 5 & 14).

(3) WHITE LAW 1,407 feet. The name, one can only surmise, originates from the vegetation that covers the upper slopes. Much of the grass on White Law is matgrass (Nardus stricta), an unusual grass that in June bears an erect unbranched spike and in late summer bleaches almost white, giving rise to the local description "White Lands", hence the name White Law.

(4) THE PENNINE WAY. Tom Stephenson, late of the Ramblers' Association was the founding father of this long distance walk way, 270 miles from Edale to Kirk Yetholm. Immortalised in the writings of A.Wainwright in his *Pennine Way Companion*, who described the traverse of the Cheviot range from Byrness to Kirk Yetholm as "the longest and loneliest of all".

(5) HALTERBURN VALLEY. This 2¹/₂ mile stretch of the valley is perhaps more familiar to Pennine Wayfarers than resident Borderers. Forlorn reminders of former days still remain in the crumbling and decaying ruins, inhabited only by itinerant sheep and noisy rooks. The walk alongside the burn is a delight, from spring to late summer flowers in bloom please the eye and brighten the day, in particular the primroses, and on the banks of the burn the musk.

WALK 5. HALTERBURN VALLEY (Cattle Grid) - WHITE LAW - BLACK HAG - THE CURR - LATCHLY HILL - WILDGOOSE HILL - SUNNYSIDEHILL - STAEROUGH HILL - HALTERBURN VALLEY

The "Halterburn Horseshoe" is a walk of 8¹/₂ miles coupled with 1,804 feet of steady ascent and descent. It stalks the Halterburn Valley on three sides over paths and trails that are easy to follow, and provides a grade 2 ridge walk of high quality in a journey time of 6 hours. Should conditions deteriorate, escape routes are at hand via the lateral valleys that feed the Halter Burn.

With the walk starting at the same point as WALK 4, cross the

Halter Burn to ascend and contour the hillside to the sheep pens. Continue up the grassy track to the Border fence, following the Pennine Way signposts south ascending steadily to White Law 1,407 feet. This summit is the commencement of the ridge which rises steadily to 1,849 feet at The Curr.

The descent south-south-east from White Law to the col below is steep but short. In wet and windy conditions care must be taken. A steady pull of 1¹/₂ miles up Steer Rig to Black Hag (1) 1,801 feet, is guided by the Border Fence. At the summit abandon the Pennine Way by turning right and descending alongside an adjoining fence, west-south-west to the col between Black Hag and The Curr. Here an escape route or easy alternative for the Pennine Way is crossed at right angles by going through the gate onto a faint trace on the left side of the ascending fence. A fence that obligingly rises west-south-west to the summit of The Curr (2) 1,849 feet.

Around the trig point on The Curr (not the most charismatic of summits), fences and stone dykes abound. The railings that descend north guide the way, with the fence on the walker's left. Immediately

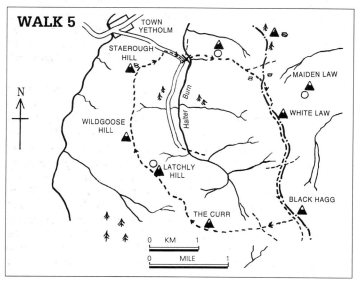

WALK 5

TOWN
YETHOLM

STAEROUGH
HILL

MAIDEN LAW

N

WHITE LAW

Halter Burn

WILDGOOSE
HILL

LATCHLY
HILL

BLACK HAGG

THE CURR

0   KM   1

0   MILE   1

ahead Latchly Hill 1,323 feet rises, its shapely slopes fully skirted in bracken, and to the west tantalising glimpses, via The Curr Burn, of the Bowmont Valley.

The saddle below The Curr leads steeply to the summit of Latchly Hill, where the path continues alongside a dry stone wall/ fence as it leads north-north-west over the western ridge. The route continues to undulate over the tops of Wildgoose Hill 1,096 feet (with its Iron Age fort), and Sunnyside Hill 1,066 feet to the peak of Staerough Hill (3) 1,086 feet. From this final section of the ridge the walker can enjoy an eagle's eye view of the valleys of Bowmont and Halterburn. The cattle grid which marked the start of the walk can be seen east of Staerough Hill. Leave the summit via the path north to join the metalled road at the five bar gate. Once the road is reached turn right, ie. east, and descend for 300 yards to the cattle grid in the Halterburn Valley. *Food and accommodation are available in Kirk and Town Yetholm.*

Items of Interest Along the Way

(1) BLACK HAG 1,801 feet. Appropriately named, "Black" refers to the heather cover, whilst "Hag" applies to the bunkers of peat. From its summit attractive views can be seen to the south, The Schil 1,985 feet, crowned by its rocky tor and circlette of outcrops, the Cheviot and the Border ridge extending westwards for 9 miles to Lamb Hill 1,677 feet.

(2) THE CURR 1,849 feet. Flat topped and sombre it stands at the head of the Halterburn and Bowmont Valleys, its position not its form being the lure. The northern prospect is particularly pleasing as the wide and graceful sweep of the Tweed Valley meets the eye.

(3) STAEROUGH HILL 1,086 feet (pronounced Stee-ruff). Rounded and covered with vegetation on three sides, this seemingly ordinary hill displays a precipitous rock face on its western flank. Six hundred feet below the summit nestle the twin villages of Yetholm - Town Yetholm and Kirk Yetholm. Kirk Yetholm was the final permanent home in Scotland for the Faa gypsies, the royal line ending with the demise of Queen Esther Faa Blyth in 1883. Several houses on the village green bear witness to earlier residents, with names such as Gypsy Row and Gypsy Palace. Knowledgeable travellers in days

gone by gave Kirk Yetholm a wide berth, for the sight of a stranger aroused the cry "oot aik sticks and bull pups". Nor was there any love lost between the two Yetholms, and even today "Yetholm Cleeks" still adorn the walls in Town Yetholm. These relics from the past resemble vintage hickory shafted golf clubs with an extra large head, very useful for repelling intruders from that other place.

WALK 6. HALTERBURN VALLEY - BORDER FENCE - WIDEOPEN HEAD - TROWUPBURN - ELSDONBURN - ECCLES CAIRN - BORDER FENCE - HALTERBURN VALLEY

A stimulating walk offering fine views of the College Valley and the Cheviot Hills, both seen at their best on a clear day. There are no steep climbs in the 1,070 feet ascent on this 8 mile walk, complete with waymarks, and it can be completed comfortably in 4 hours. Although classed as a grade 2 walk it is recommended that walking boots be worn.

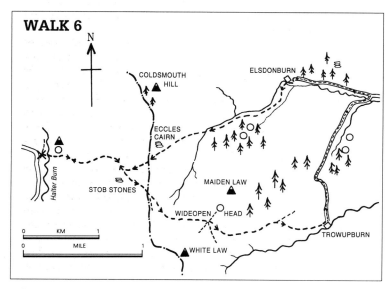

Parking is available on the grass verges close to the cattle grid at the entrance to the Halterburn Valley, GR 840277. Cross the burn east of the cattle grid, and follow the Pennine Way east-south-east, contouring the flank of Green Humbleton, as far as the sheep pens and the Pennine Way marker post. The grassy path winds as it ascends (note the Stob Stones (4) on the summit to the right), but basically it maintains the same bearing until a gate in the Border Fence (1) and another Pennine Way sign is reached. Here we leave the Pennine Way.

A good grassy track runs south-east and then east to contour the northern slopes of White Law, as far as another stone dyke complete with waymarked gate. The path holds the same bearing past Wideopen Head (a graphic description), and offers fine views of the glaciated valley of Trowup Burn. Round Madam Law 1,237 feet, and descend rapidly right of the sheep pens to the valley floor at Trowupburn (2).

From Trowupburn (a typical Border hill farm), the road winds north and then north-north-east alongside Hetha Burn, first skirting a coniferous plantation (a favourite place for the colourful chaffinch), then past ancient earthworks, to reach the bridge across Elsdon Burn 1 mile from Trowupburn.

The eastern banks of the burn provide a natural and pleasant place for a mid-walk break, and during the summer months motorists also find it a most attractive picnic spot. Five-hundred yards westwards the road brings us to Elsdonburn farm, where a waymarked arrowed route through the steading leads through two gates to open pastures. Past the second gate the track forks right and descends to cross a burn and lead into an extensive pasture field. Walk alongside the right hand fence to the northern edge of the far plantation (3). The corner of the plantation is reached via another waymarked gate, and here the path turns left between plantation and burn. Keep between trees and burn to the north-west corner of the wood, where the burn on the right is crossed by means of a simple bridge of ten railway sleepers. Once over the burn turn left and ascend south-west along the thin path, waymarked with a line of marker posts, towards Eccles Cairn (4), barely visible on the small rounded summit ahead. When level ground is reached just below the cairn bear left towards the Border Fence, which is joined at a half gate. Through the gate a faint twin track winds roughly west for 400 yards to join the Pennine Way and descend to the Halterburn Valley below. *Accommodation and refreshment available at Yetholm.*

Items of Interest Along the Way

(1) WHITE SWIRE (old spelling Swyre). The first recorded mention of White Swyre was in the 'Royal Command' of 1222 AD, when Henry III of England ordered the Bishop of Durham and the Sheriff of Northumberland "to travel to White Swyre, and there settle the Marches (Boundary), between England and Scotland, restoring them to their status in the time of King John and his predecessors". The crossing was frequently used by the Border Reivers in the 16th century. Freedom fighters or terrorists? they owed allegiance to none save their own kith and kin. Riding Families with the feared names of Armstrong, Elliot, Scott and Kerr, Hall, Foster, Charlton and Robson rode these Border crossings, especially when the moon was low in the autumn sky, and the cattle were fat and ready for the taking.

(2) TROWUPBURN (also spelt Trolhopeburn or Troughburn). The lands around this farm, in the days of the English King John, were given to Melrose Abbey by Robert Muschampe; a charter also granted the monastery's servants leave to use mastiffs for shepherding, but in doing so the dogs had to be controlled by the blowing of horns.

(3) ENCLOSURE. By Scaldhill Shank between the two present day plantations, lies this large saucer shaped enclosure. Because it is sited on lower ground it probably dates from Roman/British times, when the need for fortified settlements on high ground had diminished.

(4) ECCLES CAIRN. The burial place of a prehistoric chieftain. Unfortunately, as in so many other cases, the stones have been removed to build the dry stone dykes we see today. To the west and immediately below is Green Humbleton whose summit is encircled by the ditches and ramparts of a prehistoric encampment. Further west in the hazy distance of the Tweed Valley stand the three distinctive peaks of the Eildon Hills at Melrose, aligned precisely by the leading edge of the larger of the two Stob Stones.

WALK 7. COCKLAWFOOT - AUCHOPE RIG - RED CRIBBS - COLLEGE BURN - HEN HOLE - AUCHOPE CAIRN - CHEVIOT BURN - COCKLAWFOOT

A scenic adventure of 6 hours, carrying a difficulty grading of 4 the walk ascends 2,414 feet. Moderate to strenuous, with short sections of scrambling in the Hen Hole, the paths vary from wide grassy tracks to rough open fell. Boots, map and compass essential. In winter snow the Hen Hole can be hazardous. This 8 mile walk carries a very high rating in views and interest.

Parking is available on the grass verge, west of the wooden bridge and the ford leading to Cocklawfoot, GR 854186. Walk east through the farm yard for approximately 300 yards, with the Cheviot Burn tinkling on the left. At the first fork turn left, ie. north, to ford the burn and reach the small coniferous plantation. Pass

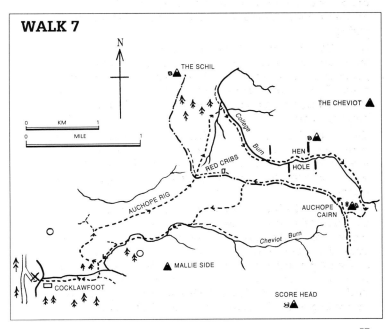

through the gate on the left, and ascend a bracken clad incline to follow the track north to two adjacent gates at the foot of Auchope Rig, GR 860196.

The grass track that travels the length of Auchope Rig ascends east and then east-north-east alongside a post and wire fence, rising 500 feet in $1^1/2$ miles, until the Border Fence is reached at GR 874202. This ridge walk affords ever increasing visual delights, with Mallie Side's ancient earthworks visible to the south across the Cheviot Valley. Beyond runs the Border ridge with Score Head, King's Seat, and Cocklawgate into England, before rising slowly and majestically westwards to Russell's Cairn and Windy Gyle 2,031 feet, the third highest mountain standing on the Border. The distinctive Schil, at 1,985 feet, fifteen feet short of mountain status, lies to the north.

When the Border Fence is reached the destination for the day is revealed. A dark and savage cleavage known as the Hen Hole (4) lies to the south-east, wedged between the rocky crags of The Cheviot 2,676 feet, and Auchope Cairn 2,382 feet. A double gate in the right angled fence allows passage to continue north-north-east, descending into the College Valley alongside the naked red earth of Red Cribbs (1). The path across heather and peat is at first faint and indistinct, but when the head of Red Cribbs is reached the narrow track on the left of the gully becomes more definite, and descends sharply into the charming alpine College Valley (2). Follow this narrow track to the valley floor, aiming between the lower corner of a coniferous plantation, a tin shed (sheep feed store) and a sheep stell. Underfoot it is inclined to be wet and boggy; note the predominance of rushes, and hopefully catch sight of a heron (3).

Once the burn and its adjoining track is reached turn south and then south-east, gradually climbing to the entrance of the Hen Hole (4). This is a good time and place to pause by the now hurrying College Burn, and enjoy your picnic amid majestic and mysterious surroundings. Once the Hen Hole is entered the ascent can be made on either side of the burn depending on ones scrambling ability. In wet or icy conditions the vegetation and dampness on the rocks can be hazardous. The way passes a charming waterfall, the Three Sisters, soon to discover two more tumbling cascades as the narrow path rises relentlessly between the towering crags, to the first of the corries on the west shoulder of Cheviot. Here the College Burn runs from the south, as the way enters a higher but smaller corrie on the south-west shoulder of Cheviot. The trace has now all but disappeared, but with the College Burn now on the left, and the summit of Auchope Cairn above, no navigation problems can arise. Once the flat floor of the corrie is reached the burn turns left, and now is the time to take a deep breath and ascend briskly due west to the summit of Auchope Cairn.

In the company of three silent "Stone Men" (cairns, which when seen from below resemble mountaineers leaning into the storm), enjoy the breathtaking views in all directions, the Tweed Valley, the North Sea and the Northumbrian Coast, the mountains of Tweedsmuir faint and far beyond the triple sentinels of the Eildons.

Descend north-west down the Pennine Way with the Border Fence on the left, to the saddle before and below the new refuge hut. A gate in the fence allows a descent southwards, to two old railway wagons and a round sheep stell on the deserted floor of the Cheviot Burn Valley. Continue west along the valley floor, frequently crossing the Cheviot Burn, to the Cocklawfoot farm track and the end of the day's walk. *A simple camp site and a farmhouse bed and breakfast are situated in the upper Bowmont Valley.*

Items of Interest Along the Way

(1) RED CRIBBS. An old drove road from the Bowmont Valley to the College Valley was described by a Warden of the Eastern Marches in 1597 as "Cribbheade - a passage and hyeway for the theefe".

(2) COLLEGE VALLEY. This most picturesque of Cheviot Valleys does not get its name from any ancient seat of learning but from the Anglo-Saxon, *Col* or *Cool*, and *Leche* meaning a bog or stream flowing through flat damp ground.

(3) HERONS. The largest bird in the Borders, these grey and graceful birds fish the burns for small trout, standing motionless on spindly legs waiting patiently to pounce.

Along the burns, usually above 1,000 feet, ring ousels can also be seen. Known as mountain blackbirds the male is black, with a distinctive crescent of white across the chest. These shy and seldom seen birds return to breed among the heather and rocks close to the mountain burns. More surprises await as we clamber deep into the Hen Hole. The cliffs and crags towering above are home to carrion crows, ravens and several breeding pairs of peregrine falcons, and until 1936 this narrow gorge was the last home in England of the golden eagle.

(4) HEN HOLE. From this lonely and lovely ravine, sculptured by the Ice Age, it is said, comes music of such sweetness that men, and women too, are lured into the Hen Hole never to return. Legend also recounts that the notorious freebooter Black Adam lived in a cave in these crags (the right-hand edge of the buttress on the Cheviot side, is today a rock climbers route known as Black Adam's Corner), and the cave could only be reached by a leap of seven paces. This wild and evil reiver received his due reward when, after raiding a wedding party at Wooperton, with the bridegroom absent collecting the Minister, he tore the jewels from the guests, then ravished and stabbed the bride to be. The returning husband-to-be, Wight (meaning strong and stocky) Fletcher, vowed revenge and gave chase through storm and darkness, relentlessly pursuing Black Adam to his lair in the Hen Hole. Finally and dramatically outside Black Adam's cave, after being locked in mortal combat, the pair crashed down the crags to the College Burn and their deaths.

> Slowly right owre then they fell,
> For Fletcher his hold did keep;
> A minute and their twa bodies
> Went crashing doun the steep.
>
> Loud and lang Black Adam shrieked,
> But naething Fletcher said;
> And there was neither twig nor branch
> Upon their rocky bed.
>
> *Anon*

WALK 8. COCKLAWFOOT - GR 860200 - SCHILGREEN - PENNINE WAY - THE SCHIL - AUCHOPE RIG - COCKLAWFOOT

Apart from the final 200 yards to the summit of The Schil, which is demanding as opposed to steep, the walk is a rambler's delight. Seven miles of upland Cheviot walking on tracks and paths that are distinct and sound; the walk can be completed in 4½ hours. Classified as grade 2, the total

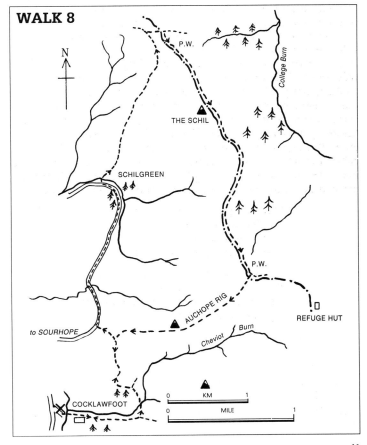

ascent of 1,263 feet is never exhausting, but always exhilarating.

Cocklawfoot (1), stands by the Cheviot Burn on the Scots side of the Border Ridge and marks the start of the walk. Parking is available on the grass verge prior to crossing the wooden bridge or the ford. Walk east past the farm steading, no doubt to the noisy accompaniment from the border collies. Swing left at the first fork, and cross the burn before reaching a small planting of conifers. Pass through the first gate on the left, ascending north up and over a bracken and rush clad pasture. The variable grass track leads to a T-junction with two fences and two gates to negotiate at the foot of Auchope Rig. Continue to walk north for 50 yards to the wide and well kept farm track at GR 860200. Turn right and follow the track north.

Any road/track that unveils the route for a distance of 2^1/$_2$ miles, through hills such as these, must rank as unique. Take full advantage of the opportunity to gaze around and drink your fill of Cheviot landscapes. Directly ahead the dark mass of Black Hag, to its left the uninspiring mound of The Curr (Walk 5), and to the north-north-east The Schil (3) 1,985 feet, crowned with a most handsome andesite coronet. On the left side of the track are the remains of an ancient homestead, later there is evidence of an Iron Age settlement. On the right a burn dances in from Birnie Brae, having gouged a deep gully into the fellside, home to countless sheep (2), moorland birds and heaths and heathers.

After a rectangular coniferous plantation is passed on the left, the track forks; carry on north, ie. right, ascending steadily for 1^1/$_2$ miles to the Pennine Way path and the Border Fence. At the Border Fence cross the stile and turn sharp right, ie. south-south-east, ascending with the fence to the summit of The Schil (3). Once on the summit, do cross the fence and scramble up the crown of rocks: 360° of best Border landscape will take your breath away.

Back to the fence, descend south-east on the Pennine Way, utilising the fence on the right as an invaluable guide for the 1^3/$_4$ miles to the gate at GR 874202. Underfoot conditions bear witness to the fact that thousands of Pennine wayfarer's boots have passed this way. The walking is good in dry conditions, perhaps not so good after periods of high precipitation. As the gate is approached the peat is forgotten, for ahead the spectacular gash in Cheviots

Sheep Half-Bred tups, Sourhope

flank, the Hen Hole (Walk 7), commands attention.

At the right angle in the Border Fence GR 874202, two gates take you through to the grassy track on Auchope Rig. A fine gradual descent south-west rambles alongside another fence for 1 mile, offering the walker an elevated display of the 5 mile Border Ridge, from Cairn Hill to Windy Gyle (Walk 10). At the foot of Auchope Rig the two gates we left four pleasant hours ago come into view, pass through, go south to the plantation and join the farm road to Cocklawfoot. The border collies will give the same vociferous greeting as they gave on departure! *Inns, B&Bs and food available in Yetholm and Morebattle.*

Items of Interest Along the Way

(1) COCKLAWFOOT. Reputed to be Hexpathgate of centuries past, a regular Border crossing for the law-makers and the law-breakers. Later this route was adapted as a local Drove Road to move cattle from the fertile Tweed Valley to the hungry markets of industrial Tyneside.

(2) SHEEP One mile to the west of GR 860200 lies the farm of Sourhope, an experimental centre of the Scottish Hill Farming

Organisation. Cheviot sheep, known previously as the Long Breed, abound on these fells. Today the breed is more compact in build, and is classed as the native or indigenous breed; others being the Border Leicester and the Scottish Blackface. Cheviot ewes when mated with a Border Leicester tup (ram) will produce a lamb known as a Scots Half-Bred. These hardy breeds living on these exposed uplands are "hefted" on to the land, ie. if the farm is sold the sheep remain. Each family of sheep, who have lived for generations on this or that particular "heft", know where to take shelter, and where the first and the best grazing lies. They also have developed an immunity to the diseases carried on their particular hillside, for every year a proportion of the ewe lambs are "kept-by/hefted" to carry on the family.

(3) THE SCHIL 1,985 feet. Stands guard at the head of the College Valley, a fitting sentinel to the most picturesque valley in the Cheviot range. Although not of mountain status this mountainous hill has a charisma of its own that draws the walker, and once on its rocky peak uninterrupted views from the North Sea to the Ettrick Forest can be enjoyed.

WALK 9. COCKLAWFOOT - CHEVIOT BURN - CAIRN HILL - THE CHEVIOT - BIZZLE BURN - COLLEGE VALLEY - RED CRIBBS - COCKLAWFOOT

Fifteen glorious miles of varied walking, over grassy paths, farm tracks, rock scrambles, peat hags, including heather louping and fording burns. An ascent of 2,674 feet over the entire walk, together with a steep descent of 820 feet by the side of the Bizzle Burn, gives the walk a difficulty grading of 4. It requires the walker to be experienced and well equipped in order to complete the round trip in 8½ hours, especially in poor visibility or winter conditions, the rewards however are high.

Leave Town Yetholm on the B6401 road for Morebattle, one mile south branch left (signposted Cocklawfoot 7 miles) onto an unclassified road, winding for 7 miles along the beautiful strath of Bowmont Water to end at the lonely farm of Cocklawfoot. Close by the farm buildings a wooden bridge and a ford signals the parking

Nether Hindhope, Kale Head (Walk 1.15)
Five Stanes Circle (Walk 1.16)

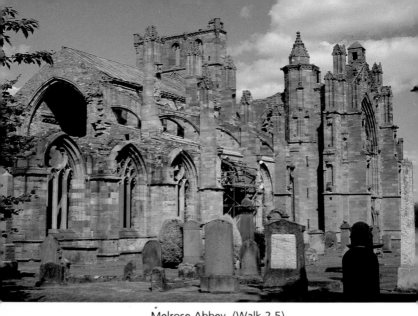

Melrose Abbey (Walk 2.5)
Peniel Heugh, Waterloo Monument (Walk 2.7)

spaces available on the grass verge.

The walk, for this the longest and the most serious of all the walks in the guide, begins at Cocklawfoot. Travel east past the farm steading to the first fork, then take the left path to cross the Cheviot Burn, a burn that will be followed to its source 2½ miles distant in the heights of Auchope Cairn. Continue past a small plantation (on the left), after which the track shrinks into a faint and wet trace, parallel with the fence on the left and the burn on the right. Ahead at the junction of two fences there is a gate, pass through and swing right, ie. east, to join a distinct farm track (this track is not marked on the OS 1:50,000 map sheet 80).

Follow Cheviot Burn east (fording it several times) for 1 mile, to a sheep shelter and two fodder stores. This restful stretch between the steep flanks of Auchope Rig and Mallie Side, with only herons and the occasional ring ouzel for company, is a delight. Several yards past the fodder stores the trail narrows and splits, take the

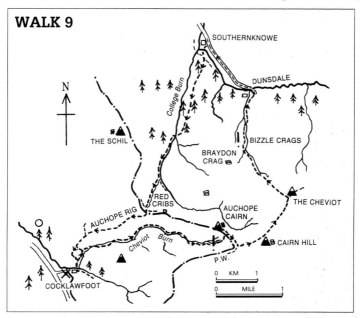

WALK 9

N

SOUTHERNKNOWE

DUNSDALE

College Burn

THE SCHIL

BIZZLE CRAGS

BRAYDON
CRAG

RED
CRIBS

AUCHOPE
CAIRN

THE CHEVIOT

AUCHOPE RIG

Cheviot   Burn

CAIRN HILL

P.W.

0   KM   1

0   MILE   1

COCKLAWFOOT

right hand fork which is now little more than a sheep track, and follow Cheviot Burn eastwards and upwards straight into the jaws of the high Cheviots. At the burnside a family of stunted rowan trees cling despairingly to the rocky outcrops, as the way heads for an open scar of bare red earth in the southern quarter of Auchope Cairn.

The ascent is now distinctly steeper, and the pathway less clear as it clings to the burnside, only to disappear once the rock scramble is met. Care and experience is needed to ascend via the route of the descending burn, for the rocks are invariably wet and in places covered with vegetation. (The gully can be by-passed by ascending the north, ie. left rim.) On emerging from the gully walk 250 yards due east across unchartered peat (beware of the wet holes), to the Border Fence, with its Pennine Way (1) duckboards. Turn right, and enjoy the duckboards, to the stile and signpost: 'Pennine Way' to the right, 'The Cheviot 1¹/₂ miles' to the left.

The peaty trench that masquerades as a path to the summit of Cheviot is initially staked with rotting marker posts. During the circumnavigation of the peat hags on this section look out for the tangled remains of an aircraft from the 1939-1945 war (2). Once the fence is reached below Cairn Hill 2,546 feet follow it east over glutinous peat to the trig point on the summit of Cheviot (3) 2,676 feet. DO NOT ATTEMPT to reach the concrete column after periods of heavy rain.

With the trig point and the fence behind the walker, set the compass to a bearing 318° magnetic (north-west), and go forth into the wilderness for ¹/₂ mile, to the source of the Bizzle Burn. At first the burn appears as a trickle, but as height is lost the volume of water increases; descend with the flow of water on the right. A second aid to the source of the Bizzle burn is the distinct rocky outcrop of Braydon Crag 2,352 feet, to the north-west. Always keep this outcrop to the left front until the burn is met.

The descent of the Bizzle Burn to the base of Bizzle Crag (4), is best tackled via the west bank of the burn. Care is needed, as the gully narrows and the burn has to be crossed several times in order to facilitate the descent. At the base of the crags the gully opens onto a boulder strewn plateau, with a path by the east side of the burn leading to the whitewashed farm of Dunsdale. The tarmac road from the farm leads first west, then north-west for $1^1/_2$ miles to Southernknowe. Turn sharp left at the farm steading, and follow the stone dyke west and then south, to a rickety foot bridge across Lambden Burn. Turn right once the burn is crossed and make for a small gap in the forest 50 yards ahead. A narrow path leads 30 yards through the trees onto a wide forest road, turn left for a few yards to the fork and then sharp right. Follow this forest road to the southern end of the plantation, leaving the trees through a small gate. Cross the field on your right to the wooden footbridge below and join the farm track south of Mounthooly farm.

It is a pleasant and leisurely walk alongside the burn to the head of the College Valley, with the gully of Red Cribbs clearly visible on the ridge ahead. This exposure of red earth is the next destination. The thin path to the skyline is joined between a block of trees to the right, and the sheep shelters to the left. When Red Cribbs has been passed and the Border Fence reached turn left towards the two gates at the T-junction, pass through and follow a good farm track by the fence, south-west along Auchope Rig for $^3/_4$ mile to reach two more gates at Auchope Rig foot. They in turn lead south through the pasture to the corner of a small coniferous plantation, passed on the outward journey. Cocklawfoot lies $^1/_2$ mile to the south-west. *Refreshments and a bed can be had in the Bowmont Valley or in Yetholm.*

Items of Interest Along the Way

(1) PENNINE WAY. Many thousands of complaining feet have pounded this section of the Pennine Way, damaging the binding vegetation on the upper surface of the peat. The result is erosion. In order to prevent further erosion, the Northumberland National Park Authority has laid sections of duckboard walkways along the worst affected parts. Centuries ago bridges were floated on bales of wool, hay or straw, and today this walkway is floated on bales of heather in an effort to stabilise and sustain the way.

(2) CRASHED AIRCRAFT. No less than nine aircraft from various air forces have come to grief on the summit of Cheviot. When the peat dries out the mangled metal skeletons rise phoenix like to the surface, only to sink again with the first rain. Bits of the metallic skeleton of a Lancaster Bomber can be seen on drier days along the western approaches to Cairn Hill.

(3) THE CHEVIOT 2,676 feet. The summit plateau consists mainly of acres of mucilaginous peat, formed because the rainwater cannot soak into or permeate the non-porous granite rock saucer of Cheviot's summit. This permanent pond prevents the heather and moss from decomposing completely, and eventually the partially rotted vegetation forms a cap of black glutinous peat. Granite also encourages the formation of an acid soil which in turn stimulates the growth of heather and ling, a cycle that does little for the walker. (See also Walk 9A.)

(4) BIZZLE CRAGS. An exposed mass of granite forms the western wall of the Bizzle, an interesting and little known cleft in the north face of Cheviot. The deep rift in the crag known as the Bizzle Chimney (rock climbers grading - very difficult) was first climbed in 1899. A word of warning, these crags can be dangerous in winter, cornices (snow overhangs) have sadly been the cause of several fatalities.

Wartime wreck on Cheviot

WALK 9A. COCKLAWFOOT - CHEVIOT BURN - CAIRN HILL - THE CHEVIOT - BRAYDON CRAG - HEN HOLE CORRIE - AUCHOPE CAIRN - CHEVIOT BURN - COCKLAWFOOT

A VARIATION OF WALK 9. This classic walk is 3¹/₂ miles shorter than Walk 9, with 668 feet less to climb. A total ascent of 2,006 feet, over 11¹/₂ miles, gives this 7¹/₂ hour journey a grading of 4. For a walk such as this it is essential to have the correct equipment, which should include map and compass. Winter walkers please ensure adequate warm clothing is worn, and emergency rations are carried. The views and interest factors command a high rating.

The starting point at Cocklawfoot and the ascent route to the summit of Cheviot (1), thence to the head of Bizzle Burn, are exactly as described in Walk 9. At the head of the deep Bizzle gully GR 904211, turn left onto one of several sheep tracks, and contour west making for the rocky outcrop of Braydon Crag, ³/₄ mile away.

Fine views to the north and north-west can be seen from the rocky perch of Braydon Crag. To the south, 200 yards beyond the

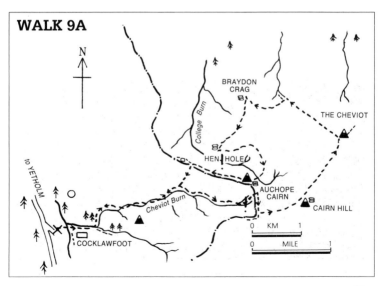

peat line, lies the grave of an American Flying Fortress B51 bomber (2), its wreckage scattered far and wide over the surrounding peat hags.

From Braydon Crags a faint track on good firm grass contours south-south-west for ³/₄ mile to the next rocky outcrop, topped by a well constructed and conspicuous cairn. The outcrop provides a fine vantage point from which to savour the dark and mysterious gorge of the Hen Hole (3), far below. Leave the crag and cairn (unnamed on the OS 1:50,000 Sheet 74) by a faint path running east and then south to contour above the corrie of the Hen Hole at approximately 2,300 feet, eventually crossing the College Burn south-east of Auchope Cairn.

It is not difficult to reach the cairn sprinkled summit of Auchope Cairn, from where fresh vistas delight the walker. The westerly descent on the Pennine Way from Auchope cairn stops at the col, before the refuge hut (4) is reached; a half gate in the fence leads to a grassy track winding south to the floor of the Cheviot Burn Valley with its fodder stores and sheep stell. The pathway winds westwards with the burn to Cocklawfoot, and the usual welcome from the collie dogs. *Food and rest as in Walk 9.*

Items of Interest Along the Way

(1) THE CHEVIOT. The area on and around Cheviot was known centuries ago as the Forest of Cheviot, within which the laws applying to wild game were enforced. All dogs, except those used for the chase, had to have one foot shortened in order to slow them down. In 1168 fines totalling 22 shillings 10 pence were imposed on local dog owners by Ralph, son of Main, for not shortening the feet of their dogs. (See also Walk 9.)

(2) CRASHED AIRCRAFT. The outer remains of the Flying Fortress are clearly visible during a dry period. Wing struts, tail fins, undercarriages, and even engine pistons still remain, although the bowels have long since been cannibalised. An attempt was made to extract one of the crashed aircraft from its peaty grave for monetary gain, using a tractor and winch. Unfortunately however, before the mission was accomplished, a storm broke and the attempt was abandoned for the day with the rescue equipment left in situ until more favourable conditions prevailed. When the bounty hunters

returned there was no sign of their equipment. Tractor and all had joined the aircraft in the peaty grave, and remain there to this day.

(3) HEN HOLE. This wild rock-bound gorge, one of the most impressive of its kind in the Cheviots, offers its crags and buttresses to rock climbers: Cannon Hole Direct 120 feet (Severe), Black Adam's Corner 120 feet (difficult), Zig-Zag (difficult), College Groves (Severe) and Long John (Severe).

(4) REFUGE HUT. The present wooden hut was constructed several years ago by a combined team of Gurkhas and RAF mountain rescue team, replacing the long standing but well worn railway waggon. Many weary Pennine Wayfarers had reason to be thankful for the old hut, as was recorded by the affectionate graffiti on its walls.

WALK 10. COCKLAWFOOT - THE BANK - BORDER GATE - WINDY GYLE - WINDY RIG - KELSOCLEUCH RIG - COCKLAWFOOT

A delightful walk along the fellways of the past, by a drovers way to the Border Gate on the national boundary, and thence to Windy Gyle 2,032 feet, one of the prime viewing sites in the Cheviots. Seven miles over easy grassy pathways (except for a short stretch on the Pennine Way), make this grade 2 walk a pleasant challenge. The ascent of 1,276 feet is never severe, and the entire circuit can be completed in a leisurely 4 hours. Walking boots are recommended.

The old drove road called Clennell Street (1) that crosses Kelsocleuch Burn at Cocklawfoot, is the starting point of the walk. Cross the bridge to the farm yard, pass through a gate then turn sharp right to a second gate shaded by a venerable sycamore tree. Initially the farm track climbs steeply to a small plantation of conifers on the immediate skyline. Go through the gate where the path slices through the trees and continue to climb and wind over the ridge of Cocklaw. Another gate is met south of The Bank 1,371 feet, and from here the path rises sharply left as it circles this sturdy buttress supporting the north side of the Border Ridge. Note the cultivation terraces to the right. Above The Bank the track levels out as the

71

Border Fence is reached at the Border Gate (2), with an attendant Pennine Way signpost and stile.

One and a quarter miles to the south-west, ie. right, the noble summit of Windy Gyle can be seen, and with the Border Fence as a guide the route is easy and distinct. The fence can be walked on either side, depending on national preference, though for the final assault the Scots side is to be preferred. A large and well formed cairn, Lord Russell's Cairn (3), stands some distance north of the boundary fence as the final ascent is made to the large and rather untidy cairn and tumulus that caps the summit of Windy Gyle (4).

A half mile descent north-west from Windy Gyle down the well trodden Pennine Way to the col of Windy Rig (aptly named), meets a small and infrequently used gate leading north onto a faint path high above Kelsocleuch Burn. As the path descends to Windy Rig it becomes more distinct, take care to use the right fork when the path splits to Kelsocleuch Rig. Ahead a coniferous plantation can be seen apparently blocking the track, once the trees are reached it

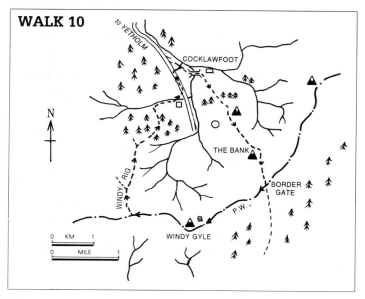

WALK 10

to YETHOLM

COCKLAWFOOT

N

WINDY RIG

THE BANK

BORDER GATE

P.W.

WINDY GYLE

0 KM 1

0 MILE 1

becomes obvious the route continues through a gate and into a wide forest ride. Take care through the ride, the way underfoot is strewn with felled branches overgrown with grass. On emerging from the trees turn sharp left to continue on a good path between a stone wall and the conifers. At the corner of the plantation by a small burn to Kelsocleuch turn right and descend with the burn as far as the farm road. Turn left to return north to the wooden bridge at Cocklawfoot. *Accommodation is available in Yetholm.*

Items of Interest Along the Way

(1) CLENNELL STREET. This street is not Roman, but an old drove road referred to in medieval charters as "magnum viam de Yarnspath", running from Yetholm and Cocklawfoot over the Border Ridge to north of Alwinton in Upper Coquetdale. Stobies 1770 map of Roxburghshire shows a road from Cocklawfoot crossing the Border at Cocklawgate leading to Upper Coquetdale, but neither this map, nor the 1st edition of the Ordnance Survey map in 1863, marks Clennell Street as a drove road.

(2) BORDER GATE. Known also as Cocklawgate and in medieval times as Hexpethgate, this Border crossing was a meeting place of the Wardens of the Middle Marches. Wardens from both sides of the Border met occasionally, as opposed to regularly, during the fifteenth and sixteenth centuries. Six wardens were appointed to administer law and order, three from England and three from Scotland, and with few exceptions the appointments were made on the principle that the most active poacher makes the best gamekeeper.

(3) LORD RUSSELL'S CAIRN. Standing below the summit of Windy Gyle to the east, the tidy cairn seen several yards north of the Border Fence. Somewhere between that cairn and Hexpathgate, during a warden's meeting in the summer of 1585 (a year of Border 'Decaie'), Lord Russell was shot and mortally wounded. He was accompanying his father-in-law John Forster, the English warden, when, according to Forster, there was some "lyttle pyckery between the rascalles of Scotlande and Englande". Suddenly a shot rang out and Russell fell. Scant consolation for the unfortunate Lord, that he remains one of the few Borderers who has a local landmark named after him.

(4) WINDY GYLE 2,032 feet. The third highest mountain actually to straddle the Border, Windy Gyle carries a large collection of broken rocks and is topped by the starred symbol of a tumulus. The site is thought to be the burial place of Iron Age chieftains. As a viewing platform it has few rivals, offering when the air is clear 360° views of the Northumbria coast, the northern Pennines, the English Lakes, the Cheviots, Tweeddale and the Southern Uplands.

WALK 11. HOWNAM - THE STREET - CRAIK MOOR - RUINED COTTAGE - HOWNAM BURN - KERSMOOR HEAD - HOWNAM LAW - HOWNAM RINGS - HOWNAM

A 10¹/₂ mile walk over the foothills of the northern Cheviots, along ancient paths that ascend 2,309 feet to peak on the distinctive summit of Hownam Law. Six hours will complete this grade 3 walk, though a journey of 7 hours will be more fulfilling. Paths are good and clear, and walking boots are recommended.

The remote village of Hownam (1) twelve miles south of Kelso, is the alpha and the omega of this exploration into Border history. Car parking in the village is limited to the grass verge opposite the sole row of cottages (please show consideration when parking your vehicle).

Start the walk opposite the south end of the row of cottages, where a side road, GR 778192, rises east from the village. At the lone house (at present off-white) swing right to ascend with the farm track to a stunted plantation on the skyline. Continue ascending as the track turns east until a junction is reached by a gate in the stone dyke. Do not go through the gate, but continue south-west, ie. right, for the next 1¹/₂ miles. The path is good though somewhat of a switchback as it travels for 1¹/₂ miles along the old drove road called The Street (2), to a small gate on the left, GR 810182. At the gate the route leaves The Street to travel north alongside another fence, across Craik Moor for ¹/₂ mile, to its 1,496 foot summit. In addition to the rolling ridges on all sides, keep a look-out for ancient marker-stones (3), spaced out at regular intervals along the moor.

Alongside a rocky outcrop on the summit, the trig point signals a sharp descent north-west, ie. left (over open fellside) to join a small burn flowing to the farm road on the valley floor. Once on the road turn left and walk west-south-west past an abandoned cottage overlooked by a solitary sycamore.

The track crosses Hownam Burn before ascending for 350 yards to meet a path on the right (*). Follow this narrow trace north by contouring the hill on the left as far as the gate, pass through, to cut diagonally across the small rough pasture to another small gate in the far corner. When the pasture has been crossed ford the burn ahead to turn right and climb north-east for 1 mile on the path to Kersmore Head 1,106 feet (bounded by conifers).

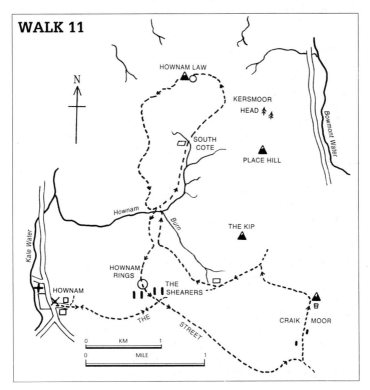

WALK 11

HOWNAM LAW

N

KERSMOOR
HEAD

SOUTH
COTE

PLACE HILL

Bowmont Water

Hownam

Burn

Kale Water

THE KIP

HOWNAM
RINGS

THE
SHEARERS

HOWNAM

THE
STREET

CRAIK MOOR

0   KM   1

0   MILE   1

The flattened peak of Hownam Law now towers above to the north, with two or three paths offering a selection of steep ascents. Take the one that looks the most comfortable, and enjoy the ³/₄ mile climb to the summit of Hownam Law (4); satisfaction and visual pleasure will be the rewards.

The descent from the south-west corner of the horizontal summit is steep and care is needed until the corner of a stone dyke is reached. From the right angle to Hownam Burn, 1 mile below, it is a steady walk alongside the stone dyke (keep the wall on your right, which for the final few hundred yards changes into a fence). Several gates have to be negotiated, as have two right angles in the dyke. Remember to walk only south or west, and keep the now empty farm of South Cote well to the left.

At Hownam Burn cross by the two marker posts and make for a gate 150 yards to the south, from there a pronounced farm track is met a further 100 yards south, where a left turn brings the walker to a fenced field. Skirt the field to a fork in the track, and take the right hand fork to the hilltop at Hownam Rings (5).

Leave the Rings on the south side of the hill. Eighty-five yards away a selection of standing stones The Shearers (6) stand straight and mysterious, inviting inspection. The path continues south for 150 yards to a gate that adjoins The Street, which is followed west as it descends the last mile to Hownam Village. *Refreshment and accommodation can be obtained at Morebattle. (For items of interest see Walk 11A).*

WALK 11A. HOWNAM - THE STREET - KERSMOOR HEAD - HOWNAM LAW - HOWNAM RINGS - HOWNAM

Should time or energy be at a premium, the ascent of Hownam Law can be included in a walk of 7 miles, with a total ascent of 1,798 feet. Omitting the ascent of The Street and the traverse of Craik Moor, the grade is reduced to 2, and the time to 4 hours.

The start is exactly as for Walk 11 over the first mile, to the gate, ¹/₂ mile past the stunted plantation. Pass through the gate and follow the grassy track east, ie. straight ahead, descending for 250 yards. At this point a faint grassy track enters from the left, ie. north (this path is clearer 100 yards ahead). We are now on the pathway to Hownam Burn and Kersmoor Head, as described in paragraph 4 (*) in the route description for Walk 11. The remainder of the route is as described for Walk 11.

Items of Interest Along the Way (Walks 11 and 11A)

(1) HOWNAM. Pronounced "Hoo-nam", this quiet village in the valley of Kale Water was, in the seventeenth century, a favourite haunt of the Covenantors. No doubt the secluded fells that surround Hownam would be ideal for prayer meetings, far away from the prying eyes of Claverhouses's dragoons. The village church has

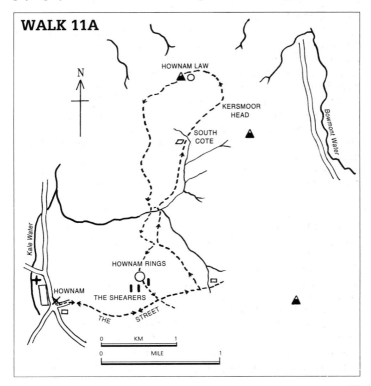

built into the south and east walls six old gravestones, an economy not infrequently met with on the north side of the Border.

(2) THE STREET. An old drove road starting in Hownam, crosses the Border at Mozie Law and runs down to Coquetdale in Northumberland. The grassy journey along its ridges provides views of high quality on both sides of the Border.

(3) ROMAN SIGNPOSTS ON CRAIK MOOR. After leaving The Street to travel north over Craik Moor, look out for several stones. They protrude two or three feet high above the ground, and can be seen on both sides of the fence. These thin post-like stones exhibit a man-made leading edge which points south-south-west to the Roman Encampment at Chew Green, some 7 miles away. The setting of this line of stone signposts is also several feet below the skyline, a well practised manoeuvre of the marching Legions: see, but not be seen.

(4) HOWNAM LAW 1,473 ft. A fine distinctive hill, whose position on the northern extremities of the Cheviots, and its loaf-like summit, make it an outstanding example of Cheviot architecture. It is generally agreed to be the best seat in the house, when it comes to viewing the Cheviots from the Scots side. The flat top of the Law is ringed in places with a massive 10 foot thick wall that once protected its Iron Age fort. Traces of the horseshoe houses within the fort can be seen in the saucer depressions.

(5) HOWNAM RINGS 1,017 ft, GR 790194. This hill fort straddles the ridge several hundred yards north of The Street. The site was excavated in 1948, and revealed a whole series of settlements, thus paving the way to an understanding of prehistoric building methods. Radiocarbon tests now show the early constructions to be sixth century BC, giving a total occupation span of 700-800 years.

(6) THE SHEARERS GR 791192. A line of 28 stones, running east to west. At present 11 of them are at ground level, the remainder stand up to 3 feet above ground. They are thought to be grounders of an ancient field-dyke of the late Roman period, not ancient standing stones, as was first thought.

WALK 12. GREENHILL GR 788176 - THE STREET - BLACKBROUGH HILL - MID HILL - HEATHERHOPE RESERVOIR - GREENHILL

An intriguing walk of 7 miles into the heart of the Cheviots, the first half swings along an old drove road, calling at two of the largest Iron Age forts in the area. The descent into the steep sided and secluded side valley above Heatherhope provides Border solitude at its best, and prepares the walker for the peaceful return along an easily walked farm road past Heatherhope reservoir to Greenhill. A 4 hour walk on dry paths, graded 2, with a total ascent of 915 feet. Walking boots and a camera are recommended items of equipment.

A single track road winds 1¹/₄ miles south from Hownam (take the left fork from Hownam), to Greenhill, standing at the junction of two typical Cheviot Valleys, Capehope and Heatherhope. Limited parking is available on the grass verge before the Y junction at Greenhill.

With Heatherhope Burn on the left, take the farm track east for 400 yards. At the bridge leave the road on a narrow pathway that ascends left, ie. north-east into a side valley. The path varies from distinct to faint as it climbs for ³/₄ mile to The Street (1). The Street

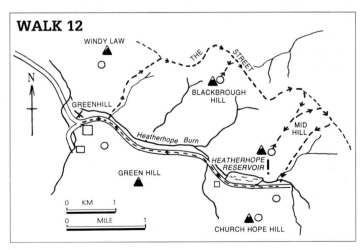

WALK 12

WINDY LAW

THE STREET

GREENHILL

BLACKBROUGH HILL

MID HILL

Heatherhope Burn

HEATHERHOPE RESERVOIR

GREEN HILL

KM

MILE

CHURCH HOPE HILL

is distinguished as the grassy track that is met forming the top of the T, turn right at the junction, ie. south-east, and ascend steadily on this grassy road for 1¹/₂ miles. The way twists in places whilst keeping to an overall bearing of south-east. When a gate in a wire and post fence impedes progress, pass through the gate and immediately turn right, to follow a thin trace through the heather parallel to a newly found fence.

Five hundred yards south-west from the gate, the impressive remains of an Iron Age fort perch strategically on Blackbrough Hill (2) 1,362 feet. After inspecting the extensive earthworks of the fort, return to The Street. Turn right and continue basically south-east; after descending for ¹/₂ mile the path splits and as if to confuse the walker proceeds on both sides of the fence, keep on the track on the right side. This ascent is through heather, and on reaching flatter ground turn right, ie. south-west, and contour for ¹/₂ mile to the summit of the ridge above Heatherhope, where further remains of an Iron Age fort and settlement (3) are evident.

Leave the fort and contour north-east along the southern edge of the ridge until the fence guiding The Street is in sight. Swing right along the fence towards Mid Hill, keeping the fence on the left. Below on the right, ie. the south-west, a steep sided valley cuts a dramatic slash between the ridge we have just visited and Mid Hill. At the end of this valley a small gate in the fence indicates a faint trace leading down the burnside. Descend south-west on this trace to the valley below, steeply at first, then a more gentle incline as the path improves, for ³/₄ mile to the Heatherhope Burn.

Surrounded by sheep shelters and fodder stores, the road winds leisurely north-west past the black waters of Heatherhope Reservoir (4), then for a further 1³/₄ miles through this forgotten valley to Greenhill. *Supplies and rest can be had at Morebattle.*

Items of Interest Along the Way

(1) THE STREET. This ancient trail ascends at length over steep sided hills from Hownam, to cross the Border between Windy Gyle and Mozie Law, journeying on over Black Braes to end its journey at the confluence of the Coquet and Rowhope Burn. It served as a drovers road for local traffic, and also had military connections. On General Roy's military map of 1755 it has the impressive name of

The Street, Hownam Rings

"Clattering Path".

(2) BLACKBROUGH HILL. A truly magnificent site for the large Iron Age fort that straddles its summit. With natural defences on three sides, in the form of steep rock and scree clad slopes, it is surrounded by an elliptical rampart 10 to 15 feet high, and is 300 yards in circumference. Minor ramparts and ditches surround the main wall, with offset openings at the two main gates. Hut circles can be seen (with difficulty), scattered inside the fort.

(3) UNNAMED RIDGE AND FORT. Matching Blackbrough as a site, this fort is not as large nor as impressive, though its population may have equalled Blackbrough. Several settlements can be found on adjacent hillocks with evidence of hut circles. Both sites were obviously important members of the network of forts that stretched across the Cheviots from Hownam Law to Coquetdale around 500 BC.

(4) HEATHERHOPE RESERVOIR. A small and now redundant reservoir, which in its heyday supplied water to the good folk of Kelso. Alongside the road to Greenhill and Hownam, spaced at regular intervals, stand cast-iron inspection valves marked "KWC" Kelso Water Company. Even now it can still be heard in certain quarters, "the waters no as guid as Heatherhope".

WALK 13. GREENHILL - THE YETT - YETT BURN - CALLAW CAIRN - GREEN HILL - GREENHILL

This walk is as lonely as it is appealing. Although classed as grade 2, it is not to be treated with disrespect, particularly on the demanding ascent to Callaw Cairn. The distance of 7½ miles, with ascents totalling 1,155 feet, provides an ideal hill walking combination of a valley walk, a challenging ascent to a rewarding summit, and finally a fine ridge walk. Paths vary though most are distinct, and navigation presents no problems on this 4½ hour trek.

Parking is available on the grass verges north of the manor house at Greenhill, at the confluence of Heatherhope and Capehope Burns. Looking south to the house the road forks; start down the right fork, over a small bridge leading to the well kept and picturesque farm steading of The Yett. Pass over another small bridge into the

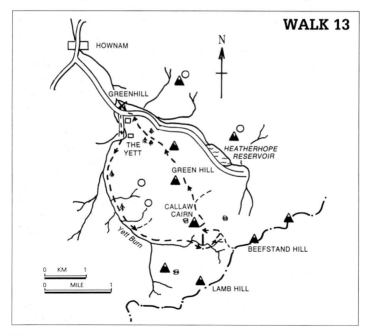

farm yard, and immediately turn right past the rockery onto a farm road. Follow this road south for $1^1/4$ miles passing two coniferous plantations, at the second the valley narrows between Whitestone Hill and Cuthberthope Rig and swings south-east.

Continue south-east to the next five bar gate, where the main track swings left and ascends steeply to the ridge. Leave the track for a narrow but distinct sheep trace to the right, winding along the valley floor with the burn. For the next mile cross the burn several times but always keep it in sight. It is on this section that the isolation of the area begins to assert itself. Above, on the ridge to the west, the abandoned cottage of Peelinick watches over the narrow valley, and to the east exposed scree covers the flanks of Thorny Hill and Callaw Cairn. The trace by the burn weaves north-east and then south-east, and the surrounding hills clamp ever closer, with the bastions of Broad Law and Lamb Hill forming a solid wall ahead. From this point on there appears to be no escape.

Yet one does remain. Between the two scree fields on the left at GR 808142 a grassy cleuch descends from the col, 500 feet above to the north-east. This ascent to the summit of Callaw Cairn (1) is demanding, but certainly not exhausting. Once on the col a fence is met running north to south; turn left at the fence, which is followed for a few yards, before climbing the final few feet to the prominent summit cairn. Pause on this top for the mid-journey break, and enjoy the sensations of space and freedom.

From the cairn descend north-east to the fence, no gate exists but a half post step eases the crossing onto a wide grassy path. Follow this path north-north-west along the ridge top for the next $2^1/2$ miles. The steady descent north-west from Green Hill (2) takes in yet another Iron Age fort, prior to entering a rather sparse collection of conifers. On leaving the trees Greenhill can be seen ahead. Walk down to the buildings, where the path winds around the east side of the steading onto a farm road and journey's end. *Morebattle is the nearest point for food and a night's shelter.*

Items of Interest Along the Way

(1) CALLAW CAIRN 1,663 feet. This distinctive hill as the name suggests, carries a well constructed and prominent cairn visible for many miles, and providing a fine vantage point from which to enjoy

the far ranging views of the eastern Cheviots. The origins of the cairn appear to be lost, though it is very likely to be the burial place of chieftains from one or more of the many Iron Age settlements and forts in the vicinity.

(2) GREENHILL RIDGE. Together with the ridge from Thorny Hill and Whitestone Hill running north-west from Callaw Cairn, the site of several large and well defined Iron Age fortified hilltop settlements. This particular section of the Cheviots was heavily populated by the Celtic Selgovae and Votadini tribes, and judging from the defensive pattern (off-set rings of earthworks) of the fortified settlements they did not live in peaceful times.

WALK 14. HEATHERHOPE - THE STREET - MOZIE LAW - BEEFSTAND HILL - CALLAW CAIRN - CHURCH HOPE HILL - HEATHERHOPE

Three miles south-east of the Cheviot Village of Hownam slumbers the dark and silent reservoir of Heatherhope, the start and the finish of this 8 mile walk. Ascending 1,171 feet, difficulty grade 2, the trek can be completed in 5 enjoyable hours. Paths are always distinct, with the ascents erring on the gentle side, though the section over the Pennine Way can be somewhat adventurous in the rainy season. Winter walks over this route are perhaps the most enjoyable, when the air is clear and the overnight snow is scrunching underfoot. Then is the time to stalk the heights of Mozie Law and Beefstand.

A narrow road runs south-east from Hownam to Greenhill, then forks left as the road surface changes from tarmac to hardcore, and narrows to single track leading to Heatherhope reservoir. Parking is available alongside the road on the slope below the north-west end of the reservoir.

Walk south-east alongside the reservoir, to pass two small feed stores. To the left an impressive valley hemmed in by steep rock strewn hills descends from The Street (Walk 12), whilst ahead the Border Ridge stands solid against the skyline and on the right the unmistakable Callaw Cairn. Cross the burn on the left at the point where an obvious path rises sharply through the heather. It winds ever upwards, first south and then east for just over 1 mile to a small gate, where it joins The Street (1). Turn right and follow this drove way for its last ¹/₂ mile in Scotland, taking care to turn right at the first five bar gate. The path soon joins the Pennine Way below Mozie Law (a seat boulder is firmly embedded in the ground at this point).

Turn right at the boulder and proceed westwards following the Border Fence, over the rounded summits of Mozie Law 1,811 feet, and Beefstand Hill 1,841 feet, on the oft trampled Pennine Way. On the western flank of Beefstand duckboards ease the passage to a right angle in the fence with an accompanying half gate. From the gate it is barely ¹/₂ mile north to Callaw Cairn 1,663 feet, on a faint path alongside yet another fence. Immediately below to the west lie the stony gorges of The Yett (Walk 13), and all around the flowing curves of the grass and heather clad hills that descend so gracefully to Tweed and Coquet.

From Callaw Cairn leave the summit by the east side to cross the

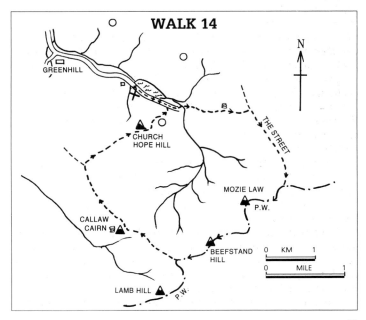

fence below, and join the pathway. Descend north for ¹/₂ mile and where the path enters a heather clad plateau swing right, ie. north-east, with the track for a further ¹/₂ mile to the pimply cairn on Church Hope Hill 1,325 feet. From here a wide and obvious path leads down to the valley floor, joining the road to the reservoir at one of the feed stores. *Accommodation is available in Morebattle.*

Items of Interest Along the Way

(1) THE STREET. A list of Border crossings compiled in 1597 included many east of Hawick, though the major drove roads crossed into England west of Hawick. Such crossings as Carter Bar (Walk 16), Dere Street (Walk 15), The Street (Walks 11, 12, 14), Cocklawfoot and Clennell Street (Walk 10), and Red Cribbs (Walks 7, 9) are all mentioned. It is more than likely that these crossings were used for local traffic, for the customs post at Kelso did little to encourage the mass movement of Highland cattle east of Hawick. The routes to the west were more private so to speak, and thus claimed the bulk of the Highland trade, as it flowed south from Falkirk. So great was the demand for Scottish cattle, that early in the nineteenth century numbers in excess of 100,000 annually crossed the Border hills, and that was only the recorded ones!

WALK 15. TOW FORD - WODEN LAW - BLACKHALL HILL - BROWNHART LAW - CHEW GREEN - NETHER HINDHOPE - TOW FORD

An informative walk, exploring the windy fells in the footsteps of the Roman Legions, along Dere Street past a Roman "artillery range" on Woden Law, to the encampment at Chew Green. A circular journey of 10 miles on good paths, where the ascent of 1,250 feet is hardly noticed. 6¹/₂ hours should be allowed for this grade 2 walk, which is high in historical and visual interest.

Tow Ford at GR 761133 stands in the Kale Water Valley, 4 miles south of Hownam. The T road junction by a cattle grid just east of Tow Ford provides parking on the grass verge for one or two vehicles, and provides the starting point for the walk. Dere Street

(1), is signposted and rises east to the col between Hangingshaw Hill and Woden Law.

On reaching the col with its stone built shed, turn right with the farm track, (the path to the summit of Woden Law (2) 1,388 feet, with ample evidence of Iron Age and Roman occupation, is 30 yards to the right), ie. south and south-east, climbing gently towards the craggy summit of Blackhall Hill 1,572 feet. The steady incline of Dere Street is indication enough, if indeed any be needed, of the skills of the Roman military surveyors and engineers.

Prior to the gate on Hunthall Hill the track branches into three; take the right-hand path through the gate to the east-south-east. Dere Street now contours above the head of Hindhope Valley, and sweeps majestically below the rocky outcrops of Blackhall Hill, (this path though perfectly safe, may cause Vertigo sufferers some discomfort; as an alternative use the ascent to Blackhall Hill), to the flat ridge of Gaisty Law. Using the marker post on the mound of Black Halls ½ mile ahead to the south-south-east as a directional

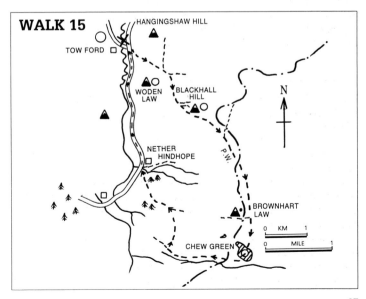

WALK 15

HANGINGSHAW HILL

TOW FORD

WODEN LAW

BLACKHALL HILL

N

NETHER HINDHOPE

P.W.

BROWNHART LAW

0   KM   1

0   MILE   1

CHEW GREEN

guide, follow the thin trace to the heather line leading to the Border Fence on the left, where a much broader track is joined. Head south with the fence to the next gate, where the signpost and well trampled path suggest the route has met with a section of the Pennine Way.

The many directional indicators between this gate and Coquet Head remove any possible navigational problems, informing us that Chew Green is 1 mile to the south. Pass the eastern flank of Brownhart Law 1,663 feet (a Roman signal station), ignore the signpost "Permissive Path, Pennine Way" that points to the right, and continue to the massive complex of Chew Green (3) on the flat lands of Coquet Head.

Leave the encampment at its south-west corner and follow the Pennine Way west for 1 mile across the damp source of the Coquet, clothed with bobbing cotton grass, to the signpost, "Nether Hindhope 3 miles". From the signpost a thin path threads its way north through windswept grasses, passing Whiteside Hill on the left, with the infant Hindhope Burn on the right. Below to the north-west a plantation of conifers can be seen, with a farm track descending alongside. Take this route to Nether Hindhope (4), and on the way glance up to the right, to the corrie of Hindhope topped by Blackhall Hill (our earlier route along Dere Street).

On the narrow metalled road it's a pleasant 2 miles walk north to Tow Ford alongside Kale Water, now flowing sedately round its ox bows, its banks heavy with Musk. *Refreshment and a bed can be obtained in Jedburgh or Morebattle.*

Items of Interest Along the Way

(1) DERE STREET. A medieval name for the umbilical cord of Roman military might, the life-line connecting Corbridge on Hadrian's Wall, to Chew Green, to headquarters Scotland at Trimontium (Melrose), and thence to Cramond on the Firth of Forth. Built around AD 80, under the command of Agricola, it has since been utilised as a drove road, and today the higher stretches are a delight to the hill walker, easing the journey and stimulating the mind.

(2) WODEN LAW, 1,388 feet. Named after a Norse God, this strategically situated hill was home to Celtic tribes during the Iron

Age. Dispossessed by the Romans, they later reoccupied the site when the Roman empire collapsed. Double ramparts and an intervening ditch surrounded the summit initially, these however partially disappeared when the Romans used the native fort for siege practice and military exercises. The precision built earthworks on the north-east corner, consisting of two banks between three ditches 40 feet to 98 feet from the original defences, are obviously Roman. In this system Roman siege machines were placed on flattened platforms on the outer bank, just beyond the range of the inner defences.

(3) CHEW GREEN. The site of an extensive Roman camp (name unfortunately unknown), built by the command of Agricola. Standing on a broad strip of open moorland near the source of the Coquet, it would be an eminently suitable site that was also easily defensible. The distinctive earthworks signify a large marching

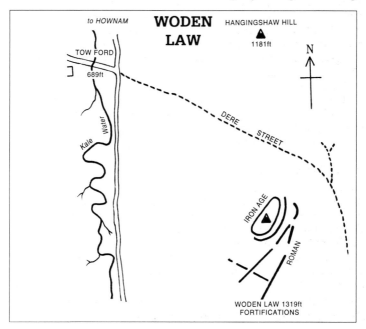

camp, a convoy post and a labour camp. Dere Street runs alongside the camp, and connects it with Brownhart Law, a signal station $1/2$ mile to the north. Chew Green later became a meeting place for Wardens of the Marches, a place to settle disputes in the violent fifteenth and sixteenth centuries.

(4) NETHER HINDHOPE. Three crossings of the Border ran south from this ancient farm to Chew Green, and in 1542 Sir Robert Bowes noted that Reivers raids caused "Brode Waies or Rakes" (broad ways or paths).

WALK 16. PENNYMUIR - DERE STREET - CHATTO CRAIG - UPPER CHATTO - WHITTON EDGE - DERE STREET - FIVE STANES - PENNYMUIR

A bright and breezy hike over the windswept fells that rise west of the once water-logged Kale Water Valley. Pathways are good underfoot, and the ascents totalling 722 feet never demanding. Graded 2, the 10 miles can be covered in a comfortable 5 hours. There is however much to see on this walk, and I would recommend a day with good visibility, as the views of the Cheviots, Teviotdale and the Tweed Valley are extensive and rewarding. Walking boots are needed for winter walking or in adverse weather conditions.

The walk starts at Pennymuir GR 755144, on the Hownam to Carter Bar Road. Pennymuir today consists of a black and red corrugated iron hut, a cattle grid and a stile, with limited parking on the grass verges by the cattle grid. Centuries ago it housed 6,000 men, and was a much grander affair (1).

Cross the stile at the east corner of the village hall, and ascend north-north-west alongside a fence and the small plantation. Approximately 1 mile along Dere Street (2) (1 mile from the start), five large stones (3) (not The Five Stanes), can be seen on the west side of the dry stone dyke. Further north on the skyline, a wire and post fence comes in from the east, ie. right. At the gate and stile in the fence turn right, and follow it east, passing through two gates. At the second gate a large and prominent standing stone (3) stands alone 100 yards to the right at GR 760157. Closer inspection reveals that its leading edge points directly north-east to Chatto Craig, topped by its Iron Age fort.

From the solitary stone walk north-east, and follow the distinct bridleway for 1¼ miles of picturesque and entertaining walking (4), past Chatto Craig 1,024 feet, to the farm of Upper Chatto. Pass through the farm steading with its white farmhouse, to descend with the tarmac road as far as the small arched bridge that crosses the Kale Water. Do not cross the bridge, but go instead due north between two stone gate posts (this roadway is a drive to a house, but it is marked as a bridleway on the OS map), turn right prior to the house through a small plantation to reach the higher ground. The farm track swings north-west over the flanks of Philogar Hill to a narrow coniferous plantation at GR 764186, at whose far end a small burn is crossed. After crossing the burn the way turns north, ie. right, for 150 yards before resuming its route north-west. The track will eventually fork, veer right, and with a burn on the right, and a

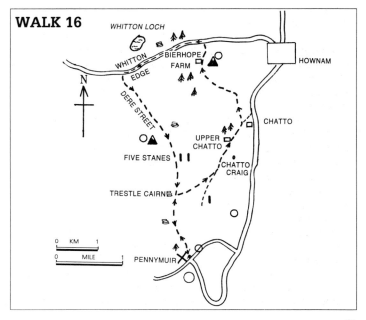

WALK 16

WHITTON LOCH

WHITTON EDGE

BIERHOPE FARM

HOWNAM

N

DERE STREET

CHATTO

FIVE STANES

UPPER CHATTO

CHATTO CRAIG

TRESTLE CAIRNS

PENNYMUIR

0 KM 1

0 MILE 1

coniferous plantation on the left, follow the track down to Bierhope farm. Continue north to join the metalled road at Over Whitton.

Ascend west, for nearly 1½ miles to Whitton Edge, noting several prominent Standing Stones (3) and the black waters of Whitton Loch lying to the north. The grass verges on this stretch of road are wide and pleasant underfoot. At Whitton Edge leave the metalled road a few yards past the cattle grid and turn south-east, ie. left, to join the straight and grassy track of Dere Street (2).

At this point it is very evident that this was a drove road of some importance, as signified by the two stone dykes lining the route, reminiscent of the green roads found in the Yorkshire Dales. In keeping with its Roman pedigree Dere Street runs in a straight line to the Standing Stone (3) on the ridge ahead (only deviating to contour any hill in its path) and is a delight to walk. On the windswept fells of Philogar, 1½ miles from Whitton Edge, stands the stone circle of Five Stanes (3), a few yards east of Dere Street. From the circle of Five Stanes pass Trestle Cairn (3) via the slowly descending Dere Street, with fine vistas to the south and east of the rolling rounded Cheviots, constantly dappled by the shadows of scudding clouds racing over the waving tussocks and the black and purple heather. Two miles to Pennymuir. *Fish and chips and accommodation can be found at Jedburgh.*

Items of Interest Along the Way

(1) PENNYMUIR. A few hundred yards south and east of Pennymuir there stood a Roman marching encampment, in the first and second centuries AD. The best preserved example of its type in Scotland, the remains of the four encampments that made up the complex can still be traced today.

Covering a total area of 40 acres, the camp could house at any one time two legions, 6,000 men, in tented accommodation.

(2) DERE STREET. This road was in use before the Roman occupation of Britain, but honed and refined by the skills of Roman military engineers and surveyors, to produce the road we now know as Dere Street. Later it was greatly favoured by drovers who walked their cattle from the Highlands and Islands, via Falkirk, eventually threading through the Borders on roads such as Dere Street.

PENNYMUIR 'MARCHING CAMP'

(3) STONE CIRCLES AND STANDING STONES. The many stones that stand lonely and sightless on these fells are thought to date from the period 2000 BC to 1000 BC, and in all probability marked the burial place of chieftains from the settlements at lower levels such as Chatto Craig. Stone circles marked these communal burial sites, the remains being interred in burial urns: "Beaker Burials". The stone circle of Five Stanes is the most complete circle on the walk, and a central point in the alignment with other similar remains.

(4) PEEWITS (LAPWINGS). Also known as plovers, these delightful summer visitors grace the fells with their distinctive cry of "Pee-Weet". Past masters of the broken wing or broken leg technique, which is used immediately should an unwanted visitor approach their nest, yet fearless in driving off predators who encroach into their territory. The "pièce de résistance" is without doubt the synchronised aerobatics of the flock, flying with such speed and precision they surely have no equal in the bird kingdom.

WALK 17. CARTER BAR - CARTER FELL - BATEINGHOPE BURN - OLD MINES - BLACK CLEUGH - CARTER BAR

The solid ridge of the Cheviot range allows but one road to cross its lonely acres; the medieval crossing of Redeswire, now known as Carter Bar 1,370 feet. Carter Bar is the start and finish of this short 7 mile walk, that runs alongside the Border, yet remains in Northumberland for its entirety. The walk traverses Carter Fell, passing five old drift mines en route, and ascends 561 feet, in 4 hours. Visually pleasing and rich in solitude, it is graded 2 in dry conditions, though in wet conditions or winter walking boots are essential.

The Border crossing at Carter Bar (1) GR 698068 on the A68 (T) road, has both parking facilities and refreshments available. Combine this, with the views and the haunting sounds of a lone piper drifting out of the nearby pine trees, small wonder dozens of touring buses pause awhile to give their occupants a chance to behold the Borderland.

Cross the road with care and walk west towards the steep, but

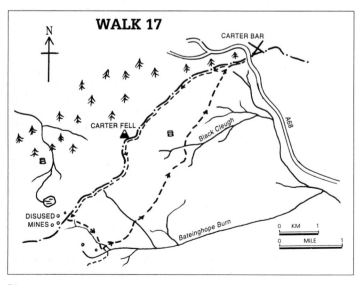

short incline of Catcleuch Shin 1,785 feet. The path marches with the fence along the south side of Wauchope Forest (now a section of the Border Forest Park). At the summit of Catcleuch Shin the hogs back of Carter Fell (2) can be seen stretching endlessly to the south-west. The Border Fence (our guide for the 2¹/₂ mile fell top crossing) runs parallel to the faint track, first south-west to the highest point of Carter Fell 1,899 feet, then after 1¹/₂ miles to a mound scattered with cairns and old mine workings, below which a small tarn nestles.

From the highest point of the mound of the mines leave the fence and walk east, ie. left across the open fell. Ahead and below, the distinct cleugh and small burn of Bateinghope slice through the heather clad peat, east and then north-east. Descend with the cleugh and the burn for ³/₄ mile until a definite pathway is met, with further mine workings (2) clearly visible. The pathway running north-north-east along the flank of Carter Fell is all that remains of what once was a well constructed mine road to and from the main road at Carter Bar. For 2¹/₂ miles this old mine road contours and slowly descends to Carter Bar, and in doing so continually delights the eye with unfolding vistas to the south and east, in particular Redesdale (3), and Catcleugh Reservoir (4). *Accommodation and food is available close by at Byrness.*

Items of Interest Along the Way

(1) CARTER BAR. This Border crossing was known in medieval times as Redeswire, a name first mentioned in the epic poem "The Brus" by John Barber in 1376. Later in 1575, as witness to the skirmish of Redeswire, immortalised in the Border ballad "Raid of the Redeswire". This site is revered every year by the good folk of Jedburgh during the Common Riding week.

> "The seventh of July, the suith to say,
> At the Redeswire the tryst was set;
> Our Wardens they affixed the day,
> And, as they promised, so they met,
> Alas! that day I'll ne'er forget!"
>
> *Anon*

(2) CARTER FELL. A dour and sombre place when the wind blows free and blustery rain lashes the face, this fell that drapes the Border.

Yet it was on the summit and the exposed slopes to the south that men laboured to win coal, and poor quality coal foreby, from its reluctant slopes. Five drift mines bored between the inhospitable cleughs and hags, and several open cast sites with their spoil heaps littering the summit, can still be seen today.

(3) REDESDALE. A valley of space and wildness, whose sons acknowledged no law and feared no one, except their neighbours, whose main interests were those of protection racketeer and reiver. Long after the country had settled down under the rule of the Tudors, Redesdale continued in its lawless ways. Today to the east of the A68 in upper Redesdale, 70 square miles of open fell is now a vast military training ground. Enormous tracts of ground are closed to walkers, with the peace and solitude that is indigenous to these hills shattered by the crump and crash of cannon.

(4) CATCLEUGH RESERVOIR. A shimmering mass of water when seen from Carter Fell, tastefully surrounded by a variety of trees, this reservoir draws its water from the isolated fells that feed the head of the Rede. Fashioned in 1905 by the Newcastle and Gateshead waterworks it supplies Newcastle and district with Border water.

WALK 18. RUSHY RIG - HARTSHORN PIKE - CARLIN TOOTH - BLACK NEEDLE BURN - KIELDER STONE - PEEL FELL - CRAIGY KNOWE - RUSHY RIG

A fascinating and varied trek through the Border Forest Park, over heathery fells and a rocky escarpment, to cleugh and gully; to the largest and the oldest "post box" on the Border. The pathways along this 12 mile circuit are as varied as the route itself. Graded 3, with 1,385 feet of ascent, the circular trek can be comfortably enjoyed in 7 hours. Mountain clothing and a compass with map are essential on this walk, particularly in winter and low visibility.

From the picturesque village of Bonchester Bridge (*refreshment and overnight accommodation available*), travel south-east for ³/₄ mile, then south on the B6357 road for 5 miles through Wauchope Forest, to the pass at Note o' the Gate (1). Here a forest road turns sharp left, ie. south-east for 250 yards, where limited parking is available on the grass verges.

The walk begins and ends on the west flank of Rushy Rig 1,365 feet, GR 590029. Follow the wide forest drive north-east for ¼ mile, veering south-east, ie. right (ignoring any paths to the left) for a further 2 miles, crossing the old road of Wheel/Whele-Causeway (1) along the way. As the trees thin the path narrows and ascends due east by a broken fence to the summit of Hartshorn Pike 1,788 feet, with fine views of Carlin Tooth, Carter Fell and Peel Fell.

The next destination, Carlin Tooth 1,808 feet (2), rises ¾ mile to the north-north-east, and is easily identified by its rocky crags and outcrops. A narrow path runs parallel to the ever present fence, but beware of the occasional wet hole in the peat, and take care when walking over the rocks on Carlin Tooth, the ridge falls steeply to the west. From the trig point continue north-north-east alongside the fence for 200 yards, then strike due east, ie. right, across open heather. On this heather clad fell there are no paths as such, and Black Needle Burn (3) appears initially as a series of wet patches surrounded by heather and peat hags. However after 500 yards from Carlin Tooth the burn takes on its true form, delighting eye and ear, as the thin trace winds with the water to join the remains of

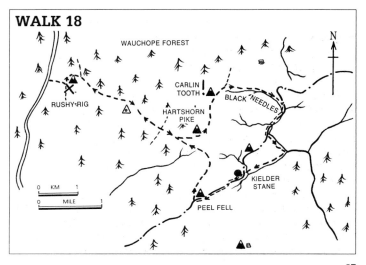

the Border Fence, first east then south, through the ever deepening gully for 1¹/₂ miles. At the junction of an unnamed feeder on the right the Border Fence leaves Black Needle Burn, and our path continues with the burn into England, where Kielderstone Cleugh (3) is joined - an ideal picnic spot, sheltered between Wylies Craigs and Upper Stony Holes.

At the junction of the two burns turn south-west and follow Kielderstone Cleugh for ³/₄ mile until a small feeder burn is reached on the left. Ascend with the feeder for 250 yards, when suddenly the massive bulk of the Kielder Stone (4) appears on the right. It is tempting but inadvisable to scale this solitary colossus, as descent is difficult and the nearest ladder is five long miles away!

From the Kielder Stone the path rejoins the Border fence to ascend steadily south-west for 1 mile to the flat summit of Peel Fell (5) 1,975 feet. The highest point of the walk, Peel Fell offers a grandstand seat from which to scan the Border hills. Leaving the Border fence and returning to Scotland, walk along the western rim of Peel Fell to Craigy Knowe 1,732 feet. On the col between Craigy Knowe and Hartshorn Pike an embryo forest road is met leading north-west; as it peters out cut across open ground to the right to join the forest road close to Wheelrig Head. This road is the one used on the outward journey. All that remains is a 2 mile forest stroll, north-west, ie. left, to Rushy Rig.

Items of Interest Along the Way

(1) NOTE O' THE GATE 1,230 feet. Centuries ago this route was one of two practical ways into Upper Liddesdale, the other, the old road of Whele-Causeway. Both routes were used frequently by the armies of England and Scotland, including Bonnie Prince Charlie and his troops in November 1745, as they journeyed south to disaster. This followed a futile recruiting drive in Kelso and Jedburgh, where not one Borderer took up arms for his cause. When the army reached the moorland pass now known as Note O' the Gate, the Prince was reputed to have heard one of his officers call to another, "Take note o' the gait" (way), thus naming the pass.

(2) CARLIN TOOTH 1,808 feet. On old maps and in old books, Carlin's Tooth. A craggy outcrop from where springs the infant Jed Water, and home to a herd of feral goats. These herds, up to 20

The Kielder Stane

strong, are descended from domesticated animals. Look out also for the mountain hares, especially in winter when they don their white coats.

(3) BLACK NEEDLE BURN, KIELDERSTONE CLEUGH. Both burns have many small waterfalls, cascading over waterworn slabs of fell sandstone into amber pools, with a profusion of flowering plants on their banks: wild thyme, catspaw, rock roses, and occasionally yellow mountain pansy. They are also home to ring ouzels (the mountain blackbird with the distinctive white flash on the chest), and the busy little dipper.

(4) KIELDER STONE 1,490 feet. Known also as Kielder Stane, this massive block of fell sandstone 26 feet high, 50 feet long and 30 feet across, is estimated to weigh 1,500 tons. Standing four square across the Border line it served during the Border Wars as a "post box". In those tempestuous times Postman Pat was not welcome on the wrong side of the Border, so messages were left in the cracks and crevices of the Kielder Stane for later collection. On its north-west corner the stone bears the inscription "ND" (the "D" in reverse), an inscription found on all the boundary stones in this section of the Borders. The letter "N" refers to the Duke of Northumberland, and

the "D" to the Douglas estate, the reverse "D" probably the work of an illiterate stone mason who inadvertently reversed the template.

(5) PEEL FELL 1,975 feet. One of the few places in Britain where a view of both coast lines is possible, and in the clear crisp air of a winter's day the northern guardians of the English Lakes Skiddaw and Blencathra can be seen, as can Cross Fell in the northern Pennines. To the east the entire range of the Cheviots as far as Muckle Cheviot, and to the north and north-west, the never ending hills of Ettrick and Yarrow and Tweedsmuir.

Chapter 2: Tweeddale and Teviotdale

THE AREA

This open Y-shaped basin of 1,870 square miles contains the valleys through which Tweed and Teviot tumble and curve to the North Sea. Ringed on three sides by solid rounded hills and rolling moors, it presents an attractive and yet dependable picture. At Kelso, where the two rivers meet, the valley widens and the graceful sweep of Tweeddale captures and holds the gaze; agriculturally bountiful and visually compelling it invites exploration. To the north the long low moorlands of the Lammermuir and Moorcroft Hills protect Tweeddale from winter's icy blasts, whilst its western flank is sheltered by the massifs of Manor and Moffat, and to the south it is supported by the ever faithful bastion of the Cheviots. The twin dales of Tweed and Teviot are, for such latitudes, green and pleasant lands.

The infant Tweed some say rises at Tweed's Wall on Tweedshaws, 9 miles north of the market town of Moffat. Others are of the opinion it springs from the loins of nearby Hart Fell 2,651 feet, and back up their theory with the old couplet,

> "Annan, Tweed, and Clyde
> Rise a' oot o' ae hillside".

Whatever spring is the true source, the Tweed flows for 98 glorious miles north to Peebles then east to Kelso, finally turning north-east to end its journey at Berwick-upon-Tweed. Its main tributary, the Teviot, trickles to life at Teviotstone on the northern flank of White Hope Edge 1,560 feet, 15 miles south-west of the mill town of Hawick, through whose marches it flows into the ever widening Teviotdale, to join the silvery Tweed at the famous salmon pool of the Junction at Kelso. Both are supported and fed by:

> "The Ettrick and the Slitrig
> The Leader and the Feeder
> The Fala and the Gala

> The Ale and the Kale
> The Yod and the Jed
> The Blackadder and the Whiteadder."

Both rivers have been at the hub of Border life for centuries, when the four great Border abbeys and their accompanying communities grew and prospered on their banks, through the bloody days of the fighting families, when the reivers built their pele towers and strongholds on both banks of Tweed and Teviot. Then, as peace slowly returned, agriculture together with the woollen industry grew, resulting in the emergence of the Border towns of today. Peebles, Innerleithen, Walkerburn, Galashiels, Melrose, St Boswells, Coldstream and Berwick-upon-Tweed all grace the banks of the Tweed, whilst Hawick and Jedburgh stand astride or close by the Teviot; only Kelso adjoins both.

Bus services connect all the towns and villages in Tweeddale and Teviotdale; timetables are freely available at bus stations and tourist information centres throughout the region.

Accommodation, ranging from hotels and inns, bed and breakfasts (in town and country), youth hostels, caravan and camp sites, is readily available throughout Tweeddale and Teviotdale, food and refreshment also. Full details are available from tourist information centres (a list of these is given in the section Useful Addresses), together with information about abbeys, stately homes, pele towers, museums (of all types), Border festivals and a comprehensive list of outdoor activities.

The river Tweed contrary to popular belief did not give its name to the world famous Tweed cloth and woollen garments, so beloved by country gentlemen and so disliked by small boys. The name "Tweed", as used when referring to the high quality cloth, came from the mispronunciation of the word "tweel", a name used in the Borders in the early 1800s to describe a local cloth; the mispronunciation, it is said, originated in London!

Dryburgh Abbey

THE WALKS

Maps recommended: OS Landranger 1:50,000 Sheets 67, 73, 74 and 80.

Each walk in this chapter is as a piece in a jigsaw, each has a separate identity, yet if all are completed the whole will provide a full and rewarding picture of Tweeddale and Teviotdale.

Walk 1 to a certain extent is the rogue of the chapter, yet the cliffs of St Abbs Head and the life on and around them are too good to miss. This coastal and cliff walk is of the highest order. By way of contrast Walk 2 starts at the "Junction" of Tweed and Teviot in the shadow of Kelso Abbey, and meanders along the river bank of the Teviot via the ruins of Roxburgh Castle to discover eventually the village of Roxburgh. High above both rivers and offering wonderful views stands Smailholm Tower, the best preserved of all the Border strongholds and the highlight of Walk 3. Walk 4 has views of the Tweed and Tweeddale that are beyond compare, as it passes by the impressive ruins of Dryburgh Abbey, a statue of a national hero, three bridges ancient and modern, and a plethora of wildlife. The triple peaks of the Eildon Hills, symbol of the Borderland, is the highlight of Walk 5, which also includes Melrose and its ancient Abbey. Walk 6 leaves the wide and fertile lower valley of the Tweed, and explores its upper reaches by means of the Minchmoor drove road and a wooded valley walk to the historic village of Traquair.

Transferring the interest to Teviot, Walk 7 is a gentle stroll to the 1815 monument on Peniel Heugh, a ridge that divides Tweeddale and Teviotdale, offering views of both. Walk 8 to the mysterious pele tower of the Turnbulls, by name Fatlips Castle, is a short walk but one to be savoured, with the sweep of Teviotdale far below. The chapter ends as it began, with a walk that perhaps geographically does not belong, for Liddesdale is a dale in its own right and its waters flow into the Solway Firth on the west coast. Walk 9 is however inexorably linked by family and blood with many of the walks in this chapter, and includes a sight of the dark and dour castle of Hermitage, whose walls have witnessed murder most foul. The circular journey over the bracing fells of Liddesdale, a stretch of historic railway line, and a druidical circle that witnessed:

> "They placed him in a cauldron red,
> And melted him, lead, and bones, and all."

is not to be missed.

INFORMATION TABLE

WALK	DISTANCE/ MILES	ASCENT	DEGREE OF DIFFICULTY*	TIME/ HOURS
1	5½	308ft	1	3½
2	9	138ft	1	5
3	3½	216ft	1	2½
4	8½	400ft	2	5
5	4	1,200ft	2	3
6	10	1,288ft	2	5½
7	4	403ft	1	2½
8	2	470ft	1	1½
9	11	1,135ft	3	6

*DEGREE OF DIFFICULTY

1 - Good path, moderate ascent, no navigational problems.
2 - Distinct path, steeper ascents, longer walk.
3 - Paths rough in places, ascent 2,000ft, exposed in places.
4 - Few paths, ascent 2,400ft plus, exposed, compass needed.

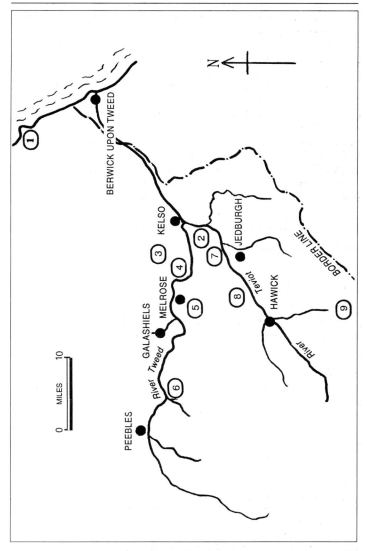

WALK 1. ST ABBS - BELL HILL - ST ABBS HEAD - PETTICO WICK - MIRE LOCH - ST ABBS - COLDINGHAM BAY - ST ABBS

A delightful and easy figure-of-eight stroll of 5¹/₂ miles, with total ascents of only 308 feet, the walk can be accomplished in 3¹/₂ hours. Striking views of and from the coastline cliffs, coupled with a unique flora and fauna, make this walk totally worthwhile. Although it carries a justifiable degree of difficulty grading of 1, do take care on the edges of the cliffs as there are no protective fences. Vertigo sufferers keep well away from the cliff edges.

The walk starts in the village of St Abbs (1). Free car parking is available in the harbour basin, and by the side of the roadway overlooking the harbour. From the harbour climb the steps to the road alongside the church, where 100 yards west a pathway turns sharp right, ie. north, with an accompanying signpost and noticeboard giving directions and details of the trail around St Abbs Head nature reserve.

Pass through two gateways to the open cliffs, then turn sharp left and follow the cliff path as it ascends along the cliff edge, before descending to sea level. Along this section seats are available giving fine views of St Abbs, the North Sea and the surrounding stacks and cliffs. At sea level a stile is met and 25 yards past the stile turn sharp right to ascend White Heugh and Kirk Hill (1). From Kirk Hill the path continues northwards, giving the first sighting of St Abbs Head, with St Abbs Head lighthouse (2) standing pristine white against the sky and the sea.

At the wall around the lighthouse turn left, and climb the small hillock on whose summit stands a directional disc and an information board. Descend from the north side passing the remains of a monastery (1) to join a metalled road. This road can be used for descent as it zig-zags west to Pettico Wick.

For those anxious to see more of the cliffs that are home to thousands of screeching sea birds (3), walk north. A westerly descent to Pettico Wick can be made down a steep grassy gully, this route should only be attempted by experienced walkers, otherwise it is prudent to return to the road.

Once the road has reached its lowest level, turn south to Mire Loch (4), cross a waymarked stile, pass beds of reeds, and take the path on the west side of the loch carpeted with primrose and violets in spring and summer, and lined with a few stunted pines and alders bent double by the winters wind (nesting sites for herons).

The path around the southern end of the loch has a fenced off area close by, marked with notices erected by the Scottish Nature Conservancy Council (3). Two hundred yards south of the fenced area the outward path is rejoined at the stile and followed to St Abbs (*refreshments and overnight accommodation*).

At the crossroads on the main street in St Abbs, high above the harbour, turn right into Creel Road and Creel Path. This pleasant agricultural walk is waymarked to Coldingham Bay, passing three hotels and the road end to Coldingham Youth Hostel (*refreshments and overnight accommodation*). At the north eastern end of Coldingham Bay (5), whose sandy beach is ringed with a crescent of brightly painted bathing huts, the path climbs many steps to a metalled pathway, returning to St Abbs.

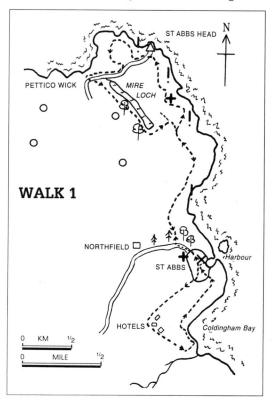

Items of Interest Along the Way

(1) ST ABBS. St Aebbe, whose seventh-century settlement was built on Kirk Hill, gave the name to the present fishing village and the rocky promontory of St Abbs Head. The remains of a monastic settlement, 70 yards by 25 yards, can be seen close by the present lighthouse, whilst to the north on the cliff edge the smaller foundations of a nunnery are just visible.

(2) ST ABBS HEAD LIGHTHOUSE. Commissioned into service in 1872, it is today unfortunately not open to the public. A radio beacon operates from the lighthouse and constant radio contact is maintained with the lighthouses of Bass Rock, Bell Rock, the Isle of May, and Fidra in the Firth of Forth. It is also a meteorological station producing weather reports every three hours. A small doubt as to the reliability of today's sophisticated equipment is raised, by the presence of a working sundial in the lighthouse garden.

(3) FLORA AND FAUNA. Covering the knowes above the cliffs sheep's fescue, red rock rose, sea pink and mouse eared chickweed grow in great profusion, with ten species of butterflies found feeding upon them. The rare northern brown argus butterfly feeds entirely on the rock rose, hence the area fenced off by the Nature Conservancy Council to prevent grazing animals eating the plant.

The cliffs and stacks of St Abbs Head are home to the largest colony of cliff-nesting sea birds on the south-east coast of Scotland. Kittiwakes and guillemots are the most numerous, followed by razor bills, shags, herring gulls, fulmers and puffins. Far below, in the foaming sea and on the rocks, live the common limpet, mussels, acorn barnacles, shore crabs and seaweed.

(4) MIRE LOCH. A narrow freshwater loch some 400 yards long, provides food and shelter for migrant birds in spring and autumn. Hundreds of gulls, fulmers and kittiwakes bathe in its waters each afternoon, after which they flutter to the east bank to preen and gossip. Swans, heron, tufted duck and coot all have a place on the loch, with goldcrest on the banks.

(5) COLDINGHAM BAY. Should the weather, and what is more unlikely the North Sea, be warm, take great care if you feel like a swim. There is a STRONG UNDERTOW ON THIS BEACH. SAFE

Mire Loch

BATHING is clearly indicated by GREEN FLAGS on the beach, UN-SAFE BATHING by RED FLAGS.

WALK 2. KELSO - ROXBURGH CASTLE - ROXBURGH - NORTH BANK OF TEVIOT - LOOP ON DISMANTLED TRACK TO ROXBURGH - KELSO

Enchanting as this walk is in all seasons, it is particularly so in the freshness of spring or in the blaze of colour that is autumn. Nine miles in total, it meanders along the north bank of the Teviot, before looping along the old St Boswells to Kelso rail-track, then returning to Kelso. An ascent of 138 feet ensures a grading of 1, and a journey time of 5 hours. Fine views of the Kelso castles, and of the peaceful river Teviot.

Start the walk at the west end of Kelso bridge (1), follow the road north by the banks of the Tweed to the junction of Tweed and Teviot. Here the road swings west alongside the Teviot for several hundred yards, before crossing over a picturesque stone bridge. A few yards beyond the cottage on the left there is the narrowest of gaps in the wall leading onto a riverside path. As the river swings west, leave the path to ascend the mound to the right, to the last few remains of Roxburgh Castle (2). From the old to the new, Floors Castle (2), colourfully embattled overlooks the Tweed to the north.

Return to the river bank and follow the riverside pathway south for 2 miles to the farm of Roxburgh Mill, the path narrows at times and several stiles (waymarked) have to be negotiated. As Roxburgh Village (3), draws nearer, the distinct but now redundant railway bridge can be seen rising high above the Teviot. At Roxburgh Mill the riverside path joins a narrow road leading to the village (3). Keep left to return to the riverside directly beneath the west end of the bridge where a small footbridge is strapped to the huge uprights.

From the bridge continue along the west side of the river bank for 1 mile. Here the river loops to the right, and the old railway track can be seen 50 yards to the right through the trees (this is a most suitable spot to take the mid-walk break). Leave the river and join

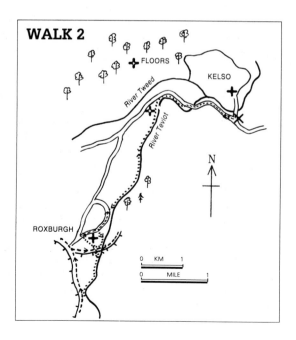

the old railway track through the gate, turn right, ie. north, and follow the route of the old steam trains to Roxburgh and the bridge crossing the Teviot. Once on the east side of the Teviot descend to the riverside to cross by means of the suspended footbridge, and walk into the village of Roxburgh (3).

From Roxburgh Mill farm return to Kelso along the north bank of the Teviot on the outward path, noting the profusion of bird life along the way. The views of Kelso are particularly pleasing when the route leaves the river bank and approaches the end of the walk. *Hotels, inns and B&Bs in Kelso.*

Items of Interest Along the Way

(1) KELSO BRIDGE. Designed in 1800, by the Scots engineer John Rennie, as the prototype for his larger creation, Waterloo bridge across the Thames (now demolished, but its lamps live on, on the parapets of Kelso bridge). This pleasing bridge has five arches with paired columns, and a classical Toll House. Grooves in the parapet nearby are said to have been made by travellers reluctant to pay the toll, so they rubbed their coins down before paying their tax - nothing changes! (Chapter 5, Kelso Town Trail.)

(2) ROXBURGH CASTLE, FLOORS CASTLE. A few walls are all that remains of Roxburgh Castle today. Built on the grassy ridge between the Tweed and the Teviot it was thought to be impregnable. Once a royal residence, it guarded the royal burgh of Roxburgh (a different site from the present village). Continually under siege, and frequently changing hands in the Middle Ages, it fell to the English, who held it for nearly 100 years until 1460. James II of Scotland, whilst laying siege to the castle, was killed by a "misframit gun" that exploded during inspection, "mair curieous nor becam him or the majestie of ane King". His queen, undeterred by his untimely demise, captured the castle, and as if to wipe the memory of this troublesome castle from her mind, ordered it to be thrown down and made completely untenable; and so it remains. Floors Castle has no such history, but remains desirably tenable. The seat of the Dukes of Roxburghe, it was designed in 1718 and completed in 1721. Then extended to the present imposing building by W.H.Playfair from 1841 to 1849.

Floors Castle

(3) ROXBURGH. The church was built in 1752, and has since been restored. In the churchyard Andrew Gemmels rests in peace. He died in 1793 at the age of 106, the original of Walter Scott's Edie Ochiltree in "The Antiquary".

WALK 3. SMAILHOLM - WESTFIELD - SMAILHOLM TOWER - MEINS PLANTATION - SMAILHOLM

A ramble of 3¹/₂ miles along quiet country roads and farm tracks to the best preserved of all the Border strongholds. The ascent of 216 feet is unnoticed, as is the time of 2¹/₂ hours on this grade 1 walk. The highlight of the ramble provides ample interest for the historian and the photographer.

The small village of Smailholm (1), at GR 648364, straddles the B6397 road north west of Kelso, an ideal starting point for the walk. Limited parking is available on the verge of the side road signposted "Smailholm Tower". Leave the village on a minor road to the west-south-west, and follow its twists and turns for 1¹/₄ miles to the single storey cottage of Westfield. As the cottage is approached the Brotherstones (2), can be seen 1 mile to the west on the higher ground.

At Westfield take the farm road to the left, ie. south-east, rising gently for ³/₄ mile to the gaunt and austere Smailholm Tower (3). Perched at 680 feet above sea level on the rocky outcrops, it commands extensive views of the Tweed Valley, lower Teviotdale and the eastern and central Cheviots. Sandyknowe farm (4) lies a few hundred yards to the east of the old pele tower, and is easily reached on the farm road. Pass through the steading and follow the narrow road north-east to Meins plantation, a small mixed wood on both sides of the road.

At a sharp right angle junction in the road turn north-west, ie. left, follow the twisting lane for 1¹/₂ miles to return to the village of Smailholm. *Kelso and St Boswells both provide accommodation and refreshments.*

Items of Interest Along the Way

(1) SMAILHOLM. Is old English Northumbrian smael ham, meaning small village. A solid church nestles on the south side of the hamlet.

(2) BROTHERSTONES. Standing stones dated 2000 BC, and set as a pair 42¹/₂ feet apart on Brotherstone Hill. The larger stone to the

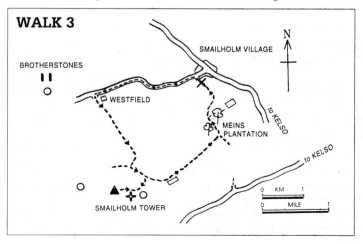

Smailholm Tower

south-east stands 8¼ feet high, its brother stands 5¼ feet high; both are supported by packed rocks at the base, and taper at the top. Lower down the shoulder of Brotherstone Hill is a much bulkier stone, 6½ feet high and known as the Cowstone. The Cowstone is aligned exactly with the two Brotherstones and Hareheugh Craigs, strengthening the theory that the Brotherstones and the Cowstone have clearly defined astronomical functions connected with the summer and winter solstices.

(3) SMAILHOLM TOWER. A fine example of a Border pele tower. First constructed in the fifteenth century, it was a Pringle stronghold, with the first recorded assault in 1546 by Sir John Ellerker, who laid siege to "Smallum towre".

Defensive rather than offensive, the simple rectangular tower of whin stone walls, 6½ feet thick, and red sandstone cornerstones, stands 56½ feet high: five storeys in all, with small windows and only a stout door on the ground floor. Surrounding the tower stands a substantial enclosing wall with a narrow gate at the west end. To the north-west stood out-buildings, built in 1650 by Scott of Harden, a direct ancestor of Sir Walter Scott.

Today the tower houses the ghosts of the past, in a fine display of Border dress, military and domestic.

Open April-September,

| Monday-Saturday | 9.30am - 6.00pm |
| Sunday | 2.30pm - 6.00pm |

(4) SANDYKNOWE FARM. Today a thriving well managed Border farm. From 1776 to 1779 young Walter Scott spent many happy months with his paternal grandfather on Sandyknowe, and it was here the seeds were sown in that most romantic of young minds. The close-by village of Smailholm is in the third canto of "Marmion", and also in the ballad of "The Eve of St John".

WALK 4. SCOTT'S VIEW - BEMERSYDE - WALLACE'S STATUE - DRYBURGH ABBEY - OLD MELROSE - LEADERFOOT - SCOTT'S VIEW

There is but one stretch of the Tweed where the silver waters weave a fabric of reflected images beneath the cliffs and overhangs, and that stretch is from Leaderfoot to Dryburgh, where stands the most haunting of all the Border abbeys. Classified as grade 2, with ascents totalling only 400 feet, the 8½ mile walk can be enjoyed in 5 hours. Easy walking on good paths and quiet roads enables the walker to wear trainers if so desired. With many high interest stops a camera is recommended.

Start the walk at Scott's View (1), GR 594342, where car parking is available. Take the road south (note the standing stone in the field on the right), to the village of Bemersyde, where a small collection of well tended cottages protect the entrance to Bemersyde House (2).

Five hundred yards south of Bemersyde the path turns right into a small copse signposted "no vehicles", and leads west for 450 yards, at which point walkers will be stopped dead in their tracks by a statue in red sandstone of William Wallace (3). Turn left at the colossus, onto a gentle tree lined path which leads south to the village of Dryburgh. Below the tiny village, on a horseshoe of the Tweed, stands the sorely mutilated remains of the Abbey of Dryburgh (4). To the west of the Abbey is an hotel, to the north a stud farm, and in the summer months an invasion of motorised travellers.

Leave the village at the post office corner, descending to the riverside and then walk west to cross the Tweed via the suspension bridge (painted British racing green). Twenty yards over the bridge turn sharp right at a yellow waymark, to zig-zag up a stepped path high above the river. Seats and resting places are scattered along this stretch for the next 2 miles, enabling the traveller to enjoy the queen of rivers.

For three delightful miles the path hugs the riverbank, crossing Bowden Burn, and following the Tweed in a series of graceful curves to Old Melrose (5). Here a line of redwoods and copper beech by the waterside indicate it is time to leave the shimmering waters and follow a farm track westwards. The track skirts the delightful trees of Ravenswood, to reach three cottages on the busy A68 (T) road. At this point the only hazardous steps of the journey are taken, but once safely across the road a wide grass verge allows safe passage for the next 250 yards, to the sanctuary of the three bridges of Leaderfoot (6). Cross by the centre bridge, an old road bridge and the most charming of the three.

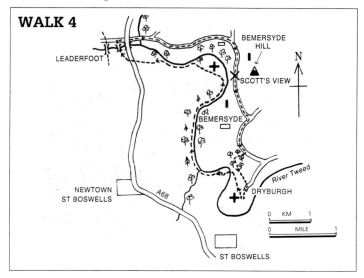

At the north end of the bridge turn right, and follow the sign Scott's View-Bemersyde-Dryburgh, crossing Leader Water to ascend the hill (look out for the plaque inset in the left-hand wall, and inscribed M M 1677), to the next fork with its guiding signpost. On reaching the fork turn right, ie. south, through an avenue of beech and oak, from where the view to the west beyond Selkirk is particularly appealing. Half an hour on the winding road returns the walker to Scott's View. *A wide range of accommodation and food can be obtained in St Boswells, Melrose and Dryburgh.*

Items of Interest Along the Way

(1) SCOTT'S VIEW. Stands at 748 feet above sea level on the western flank of Bemersyde Hill, where Sir Walter Scott, the Border's most outstanding romantic, paused many times to drink his fill. Far below, a picturesque horseshoe of the Tweed encloses the site of the Celtic monastery of Old Melrose (5), and beyond, the triple peaks of

The Eildon Hills

Dryburgh Abbey

Leaderfoot Bridge

the Eildon Hills (Walk 5, Chapter 2), spear the skyline. Lockhart, Sir Walter's son-in-law and biographer, recounts the oft repeated tale when Scott was taken to his final resting place in the confines of Dryburgh Abbey. The horses drawing the hearse paused at this very spot, as indeed they had done many times in the past. This time he was to get his final view of his beloved Borders.

(2) BEMERSYDE HOUSE. The hereditary seat of the Haig family for over 800 years. Indeed the Borders own Nostrodameus, Thomas of Ercildoune (Earlston), known locally as Thomas the Rhymer prophesied,

> "Betide, Betide, whate'er Betide,
> There shall aye be a Haig in Bemersyde".

Only the keep of the mansion is of great antiquity, a tower of the sixteenth century remains, with the bulk of the house mainly eighteenth century.

(3) WILLIAM WALLACE STATUE. Thirty-two feet high, and mounted on a plinth of local red sandstone, the inscription at his feet proclaiming, "William Wallace-Great Patriot Hero Ill Requitted Chief". Erected in 1814 by the Earl of Buchan (an eccentric member of the house of Scott), history relates Sir Walter was not best pleased by his kinsman's tribute to Wallace.

(4) DRYBURGH ABBEY. Completed in AD 1140, for and by the White Friars, during the reign of David I. It was finally sacked and brought to its knees in 1545 by the infamous Earl of Hertford, during Henry VIII's Rough Wooing of the Borders. Dryburgh fell, along with the Abbeys of Kelso, Jedburgh and Melrose. What little remained was ravaged in later years by the followers of John Knox, an act which prompted the Border prayer,

> "From all the knockdown race of Knox's
> Good Lord deliver us".

Within the shattered walls, Sir Walter and son-in-law Lockhart lie at rest, close to the Tweed and always within that sound, "the dearest of all to my ear". Only the Scotts of Abbotsford, the Haigs of Bemersyde, and the Erskines, Earls of Buchan, have the right of burial within the abbey.

Open to the public

	Weekdays	Sundays
April-September	9.30am - 6.00pm	2.00pm - 4.00pm
October-March	9.30am - 4.00pm	2.00pm - 4.00pm

(5) OLD MELROSE. Known as Mailrose, this seventh-century monastery was founded by St Aidan. Alas it is no more.

(6) LEADERFOOT. South of the leafy woods of Drygrange the Tweed is spanned by three bridges, as different aesthetically as they are functional. The oldest is the narrow and graceful road bridge built 1776-1780. Now closed to motorised traffic, but happily open to pedestrians, it was described in 1798 as "That very substantial and elegant structure over the Tweed at Drygrange whose middle

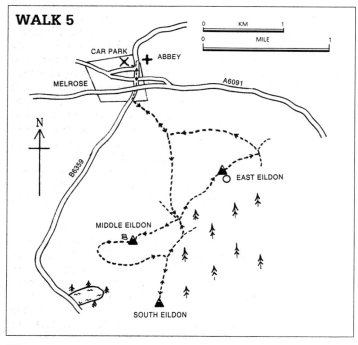

arch has a span of 105 feet". West of the old road bridge is the lofty nineteen pillared railway bridge, distinctive in its red sandstone, built in the 1860s and opened in 1865 for the Berwickshire Railway, but sadly put out to grass when the Waverley line was closed in 1963. Today this centenarian is to receive a much needed face lift. The third and most modern bridge is the road bridge to the east, a bland steel and concrete affair, carrying an ever increasing flow of traffic along the A68 (T) road.

WALK 5. MELROSE ABBEY - PRIORWOOD GARDENS - EILDON HILLS - MELROSE

The triple peaks of the Eildon Hills stand in solitary splendour in the centre of the enclave that is the Borders; low in height yet so prominent, they unconsciously throw out a challenge to the walker. This 4 mile journey is a delightful mix of an ancient Abbey, with the steep cones of the Eildon hills providing the challenge, the views, and the isolation. Graded 2, with an ascent of 1,200 feet, and a journey time of 3 hours, the pathways are good and well marked, and can be traversed in trainers or lightweight boots.

The abbey car park in Melrose is an ideal starting point, and it is free, providing the alternative of a tour of the Abbey (1), either before or after the walk. West of the abbey lies Priorwood Gardens (2), also free and well worth a visit. A walk of 100 yards south-west opens into the triangular market place with its weathered market cross. From the opposite corner, signposted Lilliesleaf, the way passes under a road bridge, and after 200 yards a sign on the left-hand wall signals Eildon Walk. The narrow waymarked track ascends steps and stiles, and passes a water trough to reach the open fell.

Turn right at the sign "MOD Firing Range" and make for the col below the middle peak. From the saddle a choice of two paths leads to the heather-clad summit of the central Eildon. The right fork takes a slightly shorter route and rewards the walker with fine views to the north and west. Although the summit of the Eildon (3) is only 1,385 feet above sea level, the exhilaration it provides totally exonerates the hill from the lack of height. A directional disc by the trig point, though worn in places, points out the items of interest on the distant horizons.

Leave the summit and descend steeply in a southerly direction. The path through the heather is narrow and in places a little slithery underfoot (use Cauldshiel loch as a marker). Once the flatter ground is reached, a distinct path curves east and then south, ie. right, to the heather covered top of the lowest Eildon, 1,216 feet. Even from this modest height the views across the Tweed Valley to the Cheviots beyond are most rewarding.

Return towards the central peak on the distinct heathery path, at a cross roads of paths (complete with marker post) go straight across, then first right, to skirt the southern and eastern flank of the central Eildon as far as the col. From here the track ascending north-east to the final peak 1,327 feet, is clear and well waymarked, with fine views of the surrounding Iron Age encampment. The descent north-east from this summit is also steep, and in wet conditions the grassy path can become extremely unstable. Descend to the gorse bushes, and turn sharp left onto a narrow track to contour west and then south-west, soon to rejoin the outward path of the M O D sign. Follow the path down the steps and return to Melrose. *Food and a wide variation of accommodation are available here.*

Items of Interest Along the Way

(1) MELROSE ABBEY. Standing proudly in the front rank of Scottish monastic buildings, it was founded and endowed in 1136 by King David I, in succession to the Celtic monastery at Old Melrose. The first Cistercian settlement to be established in Scotland, it lay in the path of the English invaders, and was repeatedly devastated. Robert Bruce bequeathed not only money to restore the building, but also his heart, though no trace of the latter has ever been found. After 1385, the abbey was rebuilt under the direction of the French master mason Jean Moreau, only to be finally plundered in 1544-5 by the Earl of Hertford. An appealing selection of humorous figures adorns the exterior walls, a mason with his mallet, a cook with his ladle, and a fat monk, and high on a gargoyle a pig playing the bagpipes!

(2) PRIORWOOD GARDENS. A section of this garden is devoted to various species of apple trees, spanning nearly 2,000 years of apple growing.

Summit of the Eildons and the Tweed valley

(3) THE EILDON HILLS. Heather clad, in a landscape where the hills are mainly grass covered, the Eildons (pronounced Eeldons) are volcanic in origin. Not one area of the Borders escapes the gaze of the Eildon climber, nor is there a summit in the Borders from which the Eildons cannot be seen. Sir Walter Scott, who frequently walked his guests on the Eildons' flanks, claimed he could "point out forty three places famous in war and verse".

Below the north-east summit the ramparts of a large hill fort can be seen. Enclosing an area of forty acres, this Iron Age settlement was the headquarters of the Selgovae tribe. It has long been a mystery how so many hundreds existed on the hill top without a recognised water supply, surely it wasn't carried up the hill every day?

WALK 6. TRAQUAIR - MINCH MOOR - BOLD RIG - WEST BOLD - HAUGH HEAD - TRAQUAIR

A fine bracing walk over one of the oldest routes through the Borders, the historic Minch Moor road. Passing Minch Moor 1,860 feet, and the Cheese

Well 1,564 feet (home to the little people) along the way, later to descend to the Tweed Valley and the oldest fortified mansion house in Scotland, Traquair House. Graded 2, this 10 mile walk ascends 1,288 feet, and can be comfortably traversed in 5½ hours. Although the paths and roads are particularly good underfoot, walking boots/shoes are recommended.

Traquair (1) lies on the B709 road 1½ miles south of Innerleithen. At the Traquair War Memorial turn south onto a secondary road leading to the village hall and the school. Start the walk at the village hall (car parking alongside the building), and turn south to follow the road to the school; at the fork a Southern Upland Waymark indicates straight ahead for Minch Moor (2). Ascend steadily south-east, squeezing between the first of many plantations flanked by two stone dykes, indicating this was an old drove road of some standing. Plentiful waymarks bring the path to an open area of heather moor below the summit of Minch Moor 1,860 feet. Contour north-east to cross a small burn GR 357336, where 10 yards to the

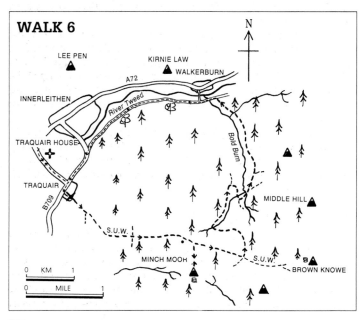

WALK 6

LEE PEN

KIRNIE LAW
WALKERBURN

A72

INNERLEITHEN

River Tweed

TRAQUAIR HOUSE

Bold Burn

TRAQUAIR

B709

MIDDLE HILL

S.U.W.

MINCH MOOR

S.U.W.

BROWN KNOWE

0   KM   1

0   MILE   1

right lies the Cheese Well (3), surrounded by heather, two marker stones and an information plaque.

Several hundred yards east of the Cheese Well turn right at the thistle waymark onto a path through the heather for $1/4$ mile to the cairn and trig point marking the flat summit of Minch Moor 1,860 feet. Spectacular views of the Manor and Moffat Hills and the Yarrow Valley. Return to the Southern Upland Way turning right between regimented ranks of the conifers. Three-quarters of a mile of gentle descent on the "thistle" path brings the walker to a wide forest road in a clearing; at this junction leave the Southern Upland Way by turning left, ie. north to descend with the wide forest road for $1^1/2$ miles. First north-west, then north along the open flank of Bold Rig, turn sharply onto the road from the right leading to the valley floor and Bold Burn. Three hundred yards along the burnside the road forks at a Water Board sign, take the left hand road alongside Bold Burn, for $1^1/4$ very pleasant miles, to reach eight wooden Forestry Commission houses at the T-junction of an unclassified road.

At the junction turn left, to follow the quiet and narrow road past West Bold towards Innerleithen; note the fine old trees on the left, and the notice stating they are managed by the Woodland Trust, with an invitation to enjoy a ramble through them. To the right the silvery Tweed hurries along the valley floor, with Walkerburn (4) across the river and the pyramid of Cairn Hill providing a distinctive backdrop.

When the B709 from Innerleithen is met, follow it south to Traquair, and the village hall. If time allows, I would strongly advise a visit to Traquair House (1), $1/2$ mile north of the village, and signposted. *Refreshments and a full range of accommodation are available in Innerleithen and Walkerburn.*

Items of Interest Along the Way

(1) TRAQUAIR, TRAQUAIR HOUSE. The name Traquair means "hamlet of the Quair". The village dating back to Roman times, was once larger than Peebles or Innerleithen. A royal hunting lodge was built on the site of Traquair House, the last monarch to hunt from there being Mary Queen of Scots in 1566. The "Bear Gates" are perhaps the most publicised feature of the house, supposedly

closed after "The 45" by an Earl of Traquair loyal to the Stuart cause, never to be reopened until a Catholic Stuart sat on the British throne. This romantic myth is however no more than a myth. The correct reason for the gates closure is that they were closed by the seventh Earl, who, after the death of his dear Countess, decreed the gates should remain firmly closed until a worthy successor was found to her.

(2) MINCHMOOR. This moorland route has been traversed for centuries by a variety of pedestrians. Monks from Kelso Abbey walked this way to their lands at Lesmahagow, Lanarkshire, in the early 1200s; in 1296 Edward I and his English army used the route to Peebles; and in 1645 Montrose's broken and battered troops staggered over its windy fells after the battle of Philiphaugh. In more recent times it has been the route for the drovers with their black highland cattle, on their way south to England via Hawick.

(3) CHEESE WELL. It has long been the custom in the Borders to keep in with a wells Fairies/Little People, by leaving a morsel of cheese to ensure a safe and successful journey, hence the name Cheese Well. Two stones by the well each with the inscription "Cheese Well" bear witness to this custom.

(4) WALKERBURN AND INNERLEITHEN. Woollen towns both, Innerleithen's first mill dates back to 1790, opened by Alexander Brodie, and Walkerburn's was opened in 1854 by Henry Ballantyne. Innerleithen proudly displays a plaque stating Robert Burns visited on 14th May 1787, perhaps to sample the waters of the oldest spa in Scotland. A printing works dating back to 1840 is open to the public. Walkerburn houses the Scottish Museum of Textiles.

WALK 7. NISBET GR 672257 - NISBET HILLHEAD - PENIEL HEUGH (MONUMENT) - NISBET MILL - GR 672257

Perched high above the Teviot, several miles north of Jedburgh, a distinctive monument thrusts skywards from the rocky outcrops of Peniel Heugh, offering fine views of Teviotdale and the Cheviots. Short in miles, only 4, this walk takes 2¹/₂ hours to complete. The ascent of 403 feet, with its difficulty grading of 1, allows the walk to be completed in light footwear, and without map and compass. Walkers with energy and enthusiasm to spare can combine this walk with Walk 8, Chapter 2, for a full and rewarding day, using the halfway village of Ancrum for food, and accommodation if required.

This pleasant walk starts at the west end of the charming hamlet of Nisbet, whose white cottages stand on the B6400 road overlooking the wide floor of Teviotdale, 2³/₄ miles east of the A68 and 3 miles north of Jedburgh. Limited parking for three cars is available at the west end of the village, on the grass verge at the junction of the B6400 and the farm road to Nisbet Hillhead.

Start this circular walk at this point, GR 672257, follow the farm road north-west as it rises steadily for 1 mile to the farm steading of Nisbet Hillhead. A short distance past the farm turn left through a gate onto a grassy path that leads to the now clearly visible monument. The summit of Peniel Heugh 774 feet, is ringed on its south and west flanks by fine tall trees, though from the rocky top the views are fortunately not obstructed, enabling the remains of two Iron Age hill forts to be seen. Half a mile from the farm the

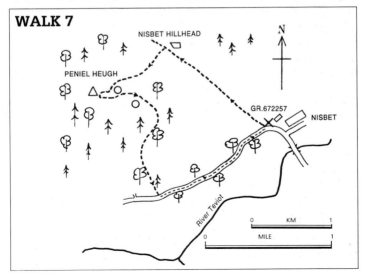

towering monument (1) rises majestically from its rocky base.

After a circular tour of the summit, and a complete external inspection of the monument (it is unsafe to enter), pause before leaving to enjoy the wide sweeps of Tweed and Teviot, ringed by the Border Hills. Leave the rocky outcrops on the south-east corner of the plateau to join a descending path into the woods, which continues south-west and then south through a finger of fine trees to join the B6400 road after ¹/₂ mile. At the road turn left, ie. east, and stroll along to the starting point through an avenue of mature oak and beech.

Items of Interest Along the Way

(1) PENIEL HEUGH MONUMENT. This spectacular round tower, topped with a wooden pagoda, was raised in 1815 by the Marquess of Lothian and his tenants to celebrate the Duke of Wellington's victory over Napolean Boneparte at Waterloo. A stout metal door prevents entry to the tower, as the structure is unsafe at higher levels. Wall plaques relate in detail the dimensions of the tower, together with the name of the stone mason from the village of Maxton. The seat of the Marquesses of Lothian, Monteviot House, lies to the south, surrounded by an impressive collection of trees that speak volumes for the estate's skills in forest management.

WALK 8. GR 585207 - MINTO CRAGS - FATLIPS CASTLE - GR 585207

A 2 mile walk with an ascent of 470 feet up the steep tree clad eastern flank of Minto Crags (1). Graded 1 for difficulty, the entire walk can be completed in 1¹/₂ to 2 hours. Lightweight boots or trainers can be worn, and a camera is recommended.

By car from the village of Denholm (2) take the road signposted Minto, cross the Teviot and take the first right turn to Ancrum. Drive 1¹/₂ miles along this road to an avenue of trees at right angles to the road on the north side, ie. left, GR 585207. Limited parking (3 cars) between the road and a five barred gate. The gate is padlocked to restrict vehicles, no such restrictions impede the walker as the path

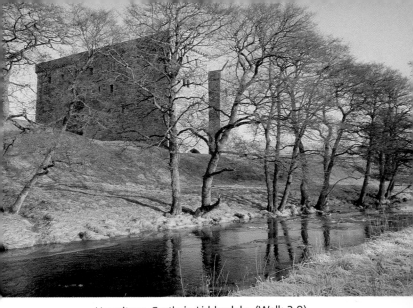

Hermitage Castle in Liddesdale (Walk 2.9)
Three Brethren and the Eildon Hills (Walk 3.1)

Dryhope Tower (Walk 3.3)
St Mary's Loch looking north (Walk 3.4)

encircles the gate to pass through a wide and airy tree lined avenue.

Two hundred yards ahead at the grassy crossroads, with Fatlips Castle (3) visible on the skyline, take the narrow path due north passing through a dense thicket of young ash and sycamore. After 20 yards the pathway swings north-east and ascends in a series of zig-zags. As with most final ascents the last few yards are the most taxing, the path narrows and twists, first between trees and finally through dense banks of stinging nettles (fortunately this is only a hazard in the late summer).

It comes as a pleasant surprise to burst out of the nettle beds to within 20 yards of this attractive, but now sadly decaying pele tower of Fatlips Castle. Due to its present unstable state a notice is displayed on the metal studded door, "Entry Prohibited, Building Dangerous". The view inside is therefore restricted to a right handed spiral stone staircase in red sandstone, a single room with a vaulted ceiling and the remains of two cannon, minus the barrels. The exterior, though crumbling in places, presents a more pleasing

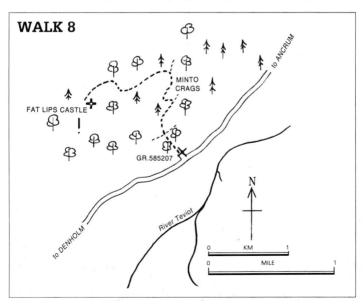

WALK 8

MINTO CRAGS

FAT LIPS CASTLE

to ANCRUM

to DENHOLM

River Teviot

GR.585207

N

0 KM 1

0 MILE 1

picture, and perched on the airy summit of Minto Crags it commands a superb vista of Teviotdale.

The descent from the tower is by the path of ascent, through this can be varied by using the steep alternative paths that descend due south. When the grassy crossroads is reached, and the final stroll is being enjoyed in the avenue of trees, glance to the right and admire the conical hill of Ruberslaw (4) as it rises in glorious isolation on the south-west horizon.

This walk could be coupled with Walk 7, Chapter 2, by travelling through Ancrum, where refreshments and accommodation are available.

Items of Interest Along the Way

(1) MINTO CRAGS. Standing 723 feet above sea level they have the reputation of being the haunt of ghosts and the Little People. It is said the first Earl of Minto walks the wooded crags at night. It is also "weel ken't" by those who know, that the fairies would carry off a child, should the simple precaution of laying the father's blue bonnet on his wife's bed be ignored. If the abduction took place after the christening, the Little People would leave another bairn in its place, invariably a "peevish, ill-thriven, wizen-faced little imp". One day a woman who lived at Minto Crag foot had carelessly forgotten to place the blue bonnet on her bed. Silently and swiftly her child was spirited away whilst she gathered sticks on Minto Crags. In the place of her bonny bairn, a "thin, wasted, wierd little creature, who yammered and wept continuously". The power of prayer, and a potion of "Whitches Thimbles" (the local name for Foxglove), both administered by the Reverend Mr Borland, minister of nearby Bedrule, fortunately restored the plump smiling babe.

(3) FATLIPS CASTLE. The stronghold of Turnbull of Barnhill, a reiver who terrorised the neighbourhood and ran a very effective "protection racket", until crushed by James IV. The grassy platform beneath the present day ruin is known as Barnhill's Bed, "Where Barnhill hew'd his bed o' flint". A painting on the ceiling of one of the rooms displayed a face with "fat lips", this may have had some connection with a previous owner and the subsequent naming of the tower, as the reivers of old were fond of nick-names, which they used frequently.

(2) DENHOLM. A charming village, *offering refreshment and accommodation to the walker,* and on whose green stands a memorial to one of its most famous sons. Son of a shepherd and a great friend of Sir Walter Scott, John Leyden was a poet (Walk 9, Chapter 2), a collector of ballads, a linguist, a professor in Bengal and a judge in Calcutta, who died at the age of thirty-six in Java.

(4) RUBERSLAW 1,392 feet. A dark and distinct hill that stands alone, short in height but strong in character, it is topped with the distinctive remains of an Iron Age fort. It also bears the "gift of Cheviot", the power to draw rain clouds to its summit,

> "When Ruberslaw puts on his cap
> and the Dunion on her hood,
> Then a' the wives o'Teviotdale
> Ken there will be a flood".

WALK 9. NINESTANE RIG - STONE CIRCLE - OLD RAILWAY (SOUTH VIA BELL HILL & BUGHT KNOWE) - ARNTON FELL - BLACKWOOD HILL - NINESTANE RIG

A fascinating walk that on a fine day unfolds the wild and isolated valley of Liddesdale. Underfoot, the 11 mile route with its total ascent of 1,135 feet, fluctuates between forest paths, a dismantled railway track, and a tramp over open fells on narrow traces. Stout footwear, suitable clothing and a map are recommended. The steep climb to Arnton Fell gives the walk its degree of difficulty grade 3, and 6 hours should be allowed for this adventure, which includes a visit to a Druidical circle and sightings of castles and pele towers most sombre.

Access to Liddesdale is not easy, as befits The Debateable Lands (1). Two roads wind in from the north, the B6357 from Jedburgh and the B6399 from Hawick. A narrow unclassified road from the A7 (T) Langholm to Hawick road winds eastwards along Hermitage Water for nine miles. Start the walk by the side of the B6399 road, 1¹/₂ miles north of Hermitage, where limited parking is available on the grass verge close to a stone built animal shelter, GR 510979.

Walk south by the roadside for approximately 200 yards towards a small bridge, on the left stands a distinct notice-board denoting the

Border Forest Park. Between the notice-board and the bridge a signpost to Ninestone Rig points south-east alongside the forest boundary fence. Ascend with the forest fence for $^3/_4$ mile to a stile leading into the trees (waymarked with the Steel Bonnet) to Ninestone Rig and the stone circle. A distinct path travels north-north-east for $^1/_4$ mile to a clearing, in which the stone circle (2) stands.

From the stone circle the path continues north-north-east between the conifers for $1^1/_2$ easy but rather monotonous miles, before descending east to the southern end of a railway cutting. This cutting is one of many on the dismantled track of the old Hawick to Newcastleton line (3).

Once on the old line turn sharp right, ie. south, for a 4 mile hike of high calibre. Never claustrophobic, even though surrounded by timber, the dismantled track reveals nostalgic memorabilia from

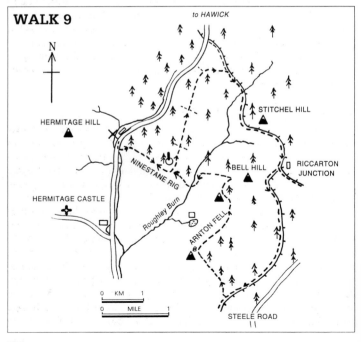

the Steam Age among the isolated remains of Riccarton Junction (3). Just past the junction the track forks, take the right fork, ie. south, then south-west for 3 miles to the boundary fence at the southern extremity of the forest. Turn sharp right at the first gate crossing the track, to ascend Arnton Fell $^3/_4$ mile north-north-west. The ascent alongside the trees is a steep plod of 672 feet, and near the crest of the fell the trees end, leaving the wall as the sole navigational aid to the summit cairn. The view from Arnton Fell exposes Liddesdale in its entirety, with Hermitage Castle (4) far below to the west on the banks of Hermitage Water.

From the summit cairn the way goes north, along the west side of a guiding wall and the rejoined conifers, for $1^1/_2$ miles to Bell Hill. As the forest turns sharp left, ie. west, the path descends steeply to Roughley Burn. Quarter of a mile above the burn the descent becomes acutely steep, and it is recommended the distinct sheep track to the left is used to traverse the hillside to the burn side. Cross the burn with care to rejoin the woodside, and passing through a small slip-rail at the corner of the trees ascend west with the fence to Ninestone Rig. The fence veers north-west, before descending to the floor of the Whiterope Valley and the B6399 road. *Services are available at Newcastleton.*

Items of Interest Along the Way

(1) THE DEBATEABLE LAND. In the fifteenth century the lands from Liddesdale to the River Sark were disputed by Scotland and England, and with neither side able to claim ownership, the rule of law was non existent, a fact quickly appreciated by the boisterous Borderers. And to make matters worse, in the 1500s the adventurous family of Armstrong produced a baby boom, spilling over into the Debateable Lands from upper Liddesdale; a powder keg situation. Both England and Scotland were then forced to take action, which they did as soon as they concluded their own war of the 1540s. In keeping with the times it was proclaimed that anyone in the Debateable Land was free to plunder, burn and kill without fear of prosecution. This fact was quickly grasped by the Scottish Warden Lord Maxwell, who in 1551 promptly ravaged the entire area, destroying buildings and a goodly proportion of the inhabitants. Forced into action in 1552, England and Scotland, with the French

Ambassador called in to see fair play, split the Debateable Land down the middle.

(2) STONE CIRCLE. A druidical circle of standing stones on Nine Stanes Rig (the old spelling), is reputed to be the place where the detested wizard Lord Soulis was rolled in lead and boiled alive.

> "At the Skelf-hill, the cauldron still
>   The men of Liddesdale can show;
>   And on the spot, where they boiled the pot,
>   The spreat and the deer-hair ne'er shall grow."
>
> *Leydon*

Two standing stones in the circle were used to suspend the fiery cauldron, and even today the vegetation within is somewhat sparse!

(3) LIDDESDALE LINE RAILWAY. From Canonbie in Cumbria to Hawick, Roxburghshire, this line twists and turns through Liddesdale to join the Bellingham to Hawick branch-line at Riccarton Junction, before diving underground at Whiterope Tunnel. Today the stripped track is there for the benefit of walkers as it winds its picturesque way to Newcastleton, 22 miles from Hawick.

(4) HERMITAGE CASTLE. This overpowering charismatic castle, greatest of all Border fortresses, dates from the twelfth century. It has in its day been held by men whose cruelty and iniquity knew no bounds. Landlords such as Soulis, Black Douglas, Bothwell and Armstrong have all left their stamp on its character. In the 1820s an outside wall was split assunder as if by the hand of retribution. Many famous visitors have come and gone, certainly the most romantic was Mary Queen of Scots, who in 1566, rode from Jedburgh to Hermitage Castle in six hours to spend a few hours with the sorely wounded Earl of Bothwell (the result of an altercation with Little Jock Elliot of Park). The Queen returned to Jedburgh the same day, and was rewarded for her concern and her efforts with ten days on her sick bed, close to death.

Chapter 3: Ettrick Forest

THE AREA

Ettrick Water and its winsome offspring Yarrow Water flow sweetly north-east through roughly parallel valleys, from Ettrick Head and St Mary's Loch, to join as one before running into the Tweed north of Selkirk. The twin glens are surrounded by a circlet of hills bounded by the old county boundary of Selkirkshire. In profile the rounded and grass covered hills resemble a herd of sleeping elephants, though the steep slopes that form the eastern wall (*) of the Moffat Water glen no doubt give another impression to walkers, who gaze up with some trepidation to the 1,500 foot rise from the A708 road.

Access to the Ettrick Forest is however good, for, unlike the Cheviots, the hills are bisected by two rivers, along whose banks a narrow ribbon of well surfaced road runs into the very heart of this delightful area. A minor inconvenience to free access onto the upper slopes being the acres of close planted conifers in both glens, and in particular in the upper Ettrick. The Forestry Commission and the private woodland owners do however permit walkers to use forest access roads and forest rides.

Whilst containing no dramatic Munroes, or even Corbetts, there are nine hills over 2,000 feet in Ettrick Forest: Herman Law, Andrewhinney Hill, Bell Craig, Bodesbeck Law, Capel Fell, Croft Head, Loch Fell, Wind Fell, and Ettrick Pen; and six tops over 2,000 feet: Trowgrain Middle, Mid Rig, White Shank, Smidhope Hill, Loch Fell West and Hopetoun Craig - a total of fifteen summits over 2,000 feet. Thirteen of the fifteen are covered in the walks in this chapter. On the heights the paths vary, ranging from distinct and good underfoot, to the faintest of sheep traces, and on some sections they are non existent. Navigation is however rarely a problem, in spite of there being a sameness about the summits and a lack of waymarks and signposts. The summits and most of the walk routes are linked by regional, county, and parish boundary stone dykes and fences which make first class navigational aids.

Not having to refer constantly to the guidebook or the map

enables the walker to enjoy the wide and varied surroundings of Ettrick Forest, ranging from the distant riot of the Ettrick and Yarrow hills, to the charm and kindly folds of the twin valleys, with the added bonus of the two sparkling jewels in the crown of Yarrow, St Mary's Loch and the Loch of the Lowes. These are quiet hills, where walks can be completed in total isolation, remaining rich in wild life both furred and feathered, and exceedingly well populated by our woolly friends.

Entry into the area is easily gained by a short drive (maximum 25 miles) from Moffat, Langholm, Hawick, Selkirk, Galashiels, or Innerleithen. Accommodation and refreshments can be obtained at several hotels and inns around St Mary's Loch, Ettrickbridge and Tushielaw, with bed and breakfasts dotted along the two valleys, as are the occasional caravan and camp sites (with wild camping possible in the upper reaches of Ettrick Water). There is also a youth hostel at Broadmeadows (the first in Scotland), 4 miles west of Selkirk, and a small "bothy" on the Southern Upland Way at Over Phawhope (Walk 9).

St Mary's Loch and the Hogg memorial

Public Transport runs through the Yarrow Valley on the Moffat, St Mary's Loch, Selkirk service. The Ettrick Valley is not so well served, Selkirk to Ettrickbridge End being the only service. Timetables are available from the bus stations and Tourist Information Centres in Moffat and Selkirk. Post buses can also be utilised in both valleys.

THE WALKS

Maps Recommended OS 1:50,000 Landranger, Sheets 73 and 79.

Walk 1 is a fine introduction to the Yarrow Valley and the surrounding hills, good underfoot with extensive views from the broad and walkable ridges, from where the route of Walk 2 can be seen covering the ridge and cirque of Sundhope and the curving flow of Yarrow Water. Walk 3 gives the walker the first sight of St Mary's Loch, then leaves the valley floor to visit two pele towers, returning alongside the musical and historic Douglas Burn.

For convenience and beauty, the next four walks all start and finish on the narrow isthmus between St Mary's Loch and the Loch of the Lowes. Walk 4 encircles St Mary's Loch visiting the old Kirk Yard of St Mary's and many other points of interest, a gentle lochside walk for all seasons. Walk 5 circumnavigates the corrie of Herman Law in its long trek over the hills that lock the head of the Yarrow Valley. Walk 6 starts as a lochside walk past the Loch of the Lowes, then ascends the high ground to the east, before descending into the Ettrick Valley. After a visit to the fascinating Ettrick Kirk it's over the hills again to return to St Mary's Loch, "That's the way for Billy and me". Walk 7 takes the route much used by Sir Walter Scott and James Hogg, when they travelled from Tibbie Shiels Inn to Tushielaw by the Ettrick, quaintly known as the Captain's Road.

The next two walks and two variations leave the lower slopes and ascend to the highest summits in the Ettrick Forest, Walk 8 covers the entire ridge above the dramatic east wall of the Moffat Water Valley (* mentioned in the introduction to Chapter 3), in addition to dropping into the head of Ettrick Water, from where the whole of the Ettrick Horseshoe, Walk 9, 9A and 9B can be seen. They are all high level walks of varying lengths, with views that surprise the visitor to the Borders, comparing favourably with some of the best in Britain. Walk 10 by comparison reveals the gentle face of the

Ettrick, and is an easy figure-of-eight walk in the land of fairies and wizards, from and to the charming hamlet of Ettrickbridge.

INFORMATION TABLE

WALK	DISTANCE/ MILES	ASCENT	DEGREE OF DIFFICULTY*	TIME/ HOURS
1	8½	1,312ft	2	5
2	8	1,226ft	2	5½
3	5½	400ft	1	3
4	7½	200ft	1	4
5	9½	1,482ft	3	6
6	10½	1,550ft	3	6½
7	12	1,660ft	2	7
8	12	2,276ft	3	7½
9	10	2,265ft	3	6
9A	6	1,170ft	2	4
9B	7	1,123ft	2	4
10	6½	490ft	1	3½

*DEGREE OF DIFFICULTY
1 - Good path, moderate ascent, no navigational problems.
2 - Distinct path, steeper ascents, longer walk.
3 - Paths rough in places, ascent 2,000 feet, exposed in places.
4 - Few paths, ascent 2,400 feet plus, exposed, compass needed.

ETTRICK FOREST

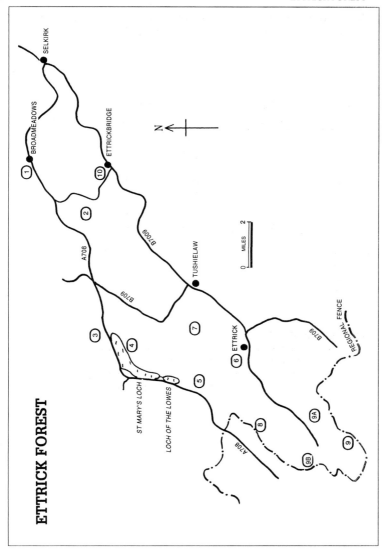

WALK 1. YARROWFORD - MINCHMOOR ROAD - WALLACE'S TRENCH - BROWN KNOWE - BROOMY LAW - THREE BRETHREN - BROADMEADOWS - YARROWFORD

Starting at Yarrowford, this introductory walk to the charm of Yarrow is all things to all walkers. Steeped in the past, with the promise of lost treasure somewhere along the way, this 8½ mile walk is graded 2, with a total ascent of 1,312 feet. Walking boots are recommended, and if the walk is contemplated in winter on in adverse weather conditions, a map and compass are advisable. In favourable weather this photogenic walk can be completed in 5 hours.

Broadmeadows and Yarrowford lie side by side on the A708, some 4 miles west of Selkirk *(all provide food and accommodation)*, involving a picturesque drive past Foulshiels farm (1), and Newark Tower (2). Parking is available at Yarrowford by the river side, close to a red telephone kiosk. Start the walk at Yarrowford by the signpost "Public footpath to Innerleithen by Minchmoor".

Pass the red village hall and several wooden garages, before entering a wood, where the farm track turns left between a corridor of oak and beech leading to the corner of Hangingshaw Wood (3).

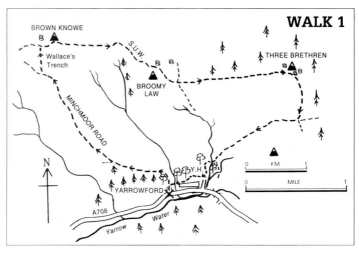

It is 2 miles from the woodside corner along the Minchmoor Road to Wallace's Trench (4). Initially the track swings north-west and follows the woodside, rising to a rig above Hangingshaw Burn and Gruntly Burn, eventually to leave the trees and zig-zag onto the open fell to the north, on what is a fine and invigorating ridge walk. As height is gained, the Minchmoor Road swings north-west as Wallace's Trench (4) is approached. A small stone marker "Wallace's Trench 300 yards", is close by the track on the right, and signals the start of this distinct trench that slashes the hillside to the north. Follow the trench to the summit of Brown Knowe 1,718 feet, turning right at the fence, onto the old drovers' road (which is now part of the Southern Upland Way (5).

From Brown Knowe follow the waymarked path (a thistle) in an easterly direction for the next 3 miles, over Broomy Law to the summit and three distinctive cairns of Three Brethren (6) 1,523 feet. This is a fine ridge walk, with extensive views of the Yarrow Valley to the south-west and the Tweed Valley to the east and the Three Brethren providing an appropriate climax.

From the Three Brethren descend south, not on the Southern Upland Way, but on the path to the right hand of the fence, walking as far as the crossroads $^1/_2$ mile below. Turn right, ie. west, at the crossroads onto a damp distinct path that loses height and crosses Long Philip Burn, before its heathery ascent south-west over the saddle, north of Foulshiels Hill. The valley of Yarrow opens up to the south-west, its silver river jinking between fold after fold of rolling hills, and fading into the distant Manor range. Continue descending for $^1/_2$ mile to the woodside by the track, here to turn right and circle the north end of the trees, by crossing a wet and boggy pasture, to the gate on the north-west corner of the wood. A waymark and a path through the mixed woods leads to the youth hostel (the first in Scotland, 1931), and onto a farm road that twists west and south for 1 mile to Yarrowford below.

Items of Interest Along the Way

(1) FOULSHIELS. Three quarters of a mile east of Broadmeadows is the birthplace of the African explorer Mungo Park (1771-1806). A man whose exploits moved Dr Livingstone to write: "For actual hardship undergone, for dangers faced, and difficulties overcome,

Mungo Park stands without a rival." A statue to this redoubtable pedestrian stands proudly in Selkirk (Chapter 5).

(2) NEWARK TOWER. Opposite Foulshiels, on the south bank of the Yarrow, stands "Newark's stately tower". Completed in 1423 "New Werk" as opposed to its predecessor "Auld Wark' was originally a royal hunting seat, the royal arms are high on the west wall.

(3) HANGINGSHAW. In the tower now long gone, dwelt the outlaw Murray. A pond or well in the vicinity of Hangingshaw is said to be the repository of a lost pay chest belonging to Montrose's army, defeated at Philiphaugh. Many have searched, but as yet none has been successful.

(4) WALLACE'S TRENCH. A single trench 300 yards long, and 4 to 5 feet deep, with the raised embankment on the west side, 4 to 5 feet high. The exact significance of this trench is not exactly clear, as it must have been constructed well before the lifetime of Sir William Wallace.

(5) SOUTHERN UPLAND WAY. A continuous long distance coast to coast path, opened in 1984, from Portpatrick on the west coast to Cockburnspath on the Berwickshire coast, it covers a distance of 202 miles (see Chapter 5).

(6) THREE BRETHREN 1,523 feet. This prominent hill stands to the north-west of Selkirk, crowned by three large identical cairns, each 9 feet tall and 6 foot in diameter at the base, hence the name Three Brethren. Each cairn marks the boundary of the estates of Yair, of Philiphaugh, and the burgh of Selkirk. The Brethren are visited on the first Tuesday of June, during Selkirk's colourful "Common Riding" festivities, when the marches are ridden and the colours are "cast".

WALK 2. YARROW - WITCHIE KNOWE - ROUGH KNOWE - LADHOPE MIDDLE - SUNDHOPE HEIGHT - SUNDHOPE - LADHOPE - YARROW

The Yarrow and its surrounding hills, it is said, have more beauty, more

standing stones and cairns, and more pure air (1), than any other area in the Borders. This 8 mile walk along the river side and over Sundhope Rig allows comparisons to be made during the ascent of 1,226 feet, with time to spot the twenty cairns and standing stones that cover the adjacent hills. Graded 2 the walk will take 5½ hours; walking boots are recommended in wet conditions. The paths vary from good farm tracks to sheep traces on the open fell.

The tiny hamlet of Yarrow lies alongside Yarrow Water between Whitehope Burn and Deucher Burn on the A708 road from Selkirk to St Mary's Loch, 8½ miles west of Selkirk. Parking is possible on the grassy triangle north of the bridge across Yarrow Water, or on the grass verge on the south side. With Yarrow Kirk and the Manse (1) behind, cross the bridge and ascend the narrow road south for 1½ miles to Witchie Knowe (2). This metalled road with passing places connects the Yarrow and the Ettrick, the grass verges at the

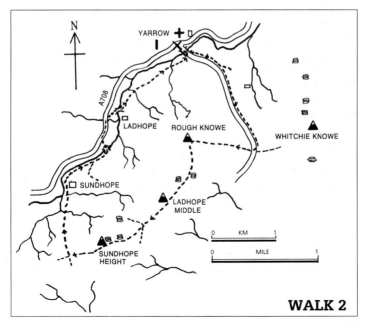

WALK 2

side of the road improve the walking as do the views as height is gained.

At Witchie Knowe, by the cattle grid, turn right and leave the road to ascend the track leading west to the summit of Rough Knowe 1,580 feet. The climb alongside the stone dyke sets the stage for a fine ridge walk of nearly 3 miles, travelling south-west, ie. left, from Rough Knowe along a thin path to Ladhope Middle 1,406 feet, and Sundhope Height 1,684 feet. This ridge is a favourite area for the mountain hare (white coat in winter), and small groups of feral goats. Sundhope Height with its cairn in close proximity, is a wonderful viewing platform and on a clear day a fine picnic spot.

One mile to the south-west on the col below Sundhope Height turn right, ie. north, to descend on what was possibly an old drove road to Sundhope farm, 1¹/₂ miles below. From the farm follow a farm track north-east, with the picturesque Yarrow Water on the left. This riverside walk leads north-east for 2 miles past Ladhope and Yarrow cottages to the east end of the bridge at Yarrow (3). *Refreshment and accommodation are available at B&Bs along the valley, and in Selkirk.*

Items of Interest Along the Way

(1) YARROW KIRK AND YARROW MANSE. As living testimony to the pure air of Yarrow, the Parish of Yarrow had only three ministers from 1791 to 1883, the Russells, father and son, and the Reverend Borland. The Kirk, built in 1640, had as its first minister the Reverend Rutherford, maternal great-grandfather of Sir Walter Scott.

(2) WITCHIE KNOWE. The story is told of a Michael Scott (who owned Oakwood Tower) and the Witch of Fauldshope (the hill close by to Witchie Knowe). "One day he burst forth from her cottage door in the guise of a hare, only to be coursed by his own hounds on Fauldshope Hill." The lady in question was an ancestor of James Hogg, the Ettrick Shepherd (Chapter 3, Walks 6 and 7).

(3) DEUCHER BRIDGE AND THE INSCRIBED STONE. Deucher bridge stood below the ruins of Deucher tower, a Scott stronghold. In 1734 the south arch of the bridge was swept away in the great flood, much to the consternation of the good parishioners of Yarrow

who lived on the south side of the river, for now church attendance meant wading through the raging torrent, no mean feat especially in winter. Marriages frequently had to be postponed, and the dead were especially inconvenienced, should they wish to be laid at rest alongside their friends and loved ones in the Kirk Yaird.

A few hundred yards south-west of the Warriors Rest at Yarrow, on the north side of the road, stand two massive unhewn stones, monuments to two waring chieftains. Their followers were not so honoured, the bodies being disposed of in the marshy pool in the neighbouring haugh, known to this day as "The Dead Lake". Three hundred yards to the west, a large flat stone bearing a faint Latin inscription was unearthed above bones and ashes. Around this find the grass grows green and lush. It is highly probable this is the locality of the poem "The Dowie Dens of Yarrow".

WALK 3. DRYHOPE - BLACKHOUSE - CRAIG DOUGLAS - DRYHOPE

So many infinitely more capable than I have in prose and verse sung the praises of this valley of Yarrow. By walking the highways and the byways, the traveller can appreciate the romance of the legends, and the beauty of its waters. This walk of 5½ miles carries a difficulty grade of 1, as good, well marked paths ease the walker over the 400 feet of ascent, on a journey of 3 hours.

Dryhope stands a few hundred yards north of the A708 road, at the east end of St Mary's Loch and 15¼ delightful miles west of Selkirk. Parking is restricted, but the verges/layby at the lochside a few hundred yards west can be utilised. The walk starts at the Southern Upland Way crossing GR 269242, marked by two stiles, from this point proceed north, with Dryhope farm on the left and Dryhope Tower (1) ahead. From the nearest point to Dryhope Tower turn right after crossing the stile, and follow the clear track between Ward Law and South Hawkshaw Rig (with its prominent cairn). After about ½ mile the farm track swings left and follows the Dryhope Burn, our route carries on north-east onto a grassy path past the cairn and a circular sheep stell to a split in the path. Take the left fork to a waymark below, keeping north-east past more waymarks (the thistle), towards a line of silver birches in Hawkshaw Cleuch. The path widens as it ascends to a bridge; after crossing the bridge follow a fence on the right as far as the next waymark. At this point leave the fence via a descending trail to a wooden bridge over the Douglas Burn to Blackhouse (2).

Nestling in the confluence of the Douglas Burn (3) and Craighope Burn, and below the steep side of Whitehope Rig 1,587 feet, stand the few remains of Blackhouse Tower, close by the working farm of Blackhouse. Once across the Douglas Burn turn right and follow the farm track south for 2 miles to Craig Douglas. The winding track keeps close to the burn, which is a pandora's box of birdlife (4) and wild flowers. The farm of Craig Douglas is white and tidy as it stands close by the A708, with its milestone on the south side of the road. Turn right onto the road, which is followed west for 1¹/₂ miles to the Southern Upland Way crossing at Dryhope. *Food and accommodation can be had at various hotels and inns around St Mary's*

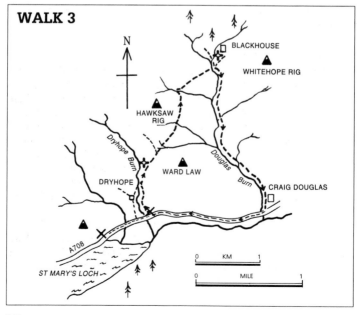

WALK 3

N

BLACKHOUSE

WHITEHOPE RIG

HAWKSAW RIG

Dryhope Burn

Douglas Burn

WARD LAW

DRYHOPE

CRAIG DOUGLAS

A708

ST MARY'S LOCH

| 0 | KM | 1 |
| 0 | MILE | 1 |

Dryhope Tower

Loch or B&Bs along the Yarrow. There is also the youth hostel at Broadmeadows.

Items of Interest Along the Way

(1) DRYHOPE TOWER. This massive little pele tower (10 yards by 7 yards, with walls 3 feet thick), was the birthplace in 1550 of Mary the Flower of Yarrow, bride of Auld Wat Scott of Harden. As if the tenancy of a Scott of Auld Wat's calibre was not enough, the tower was also home to another brigand of great notoriety. Dick of Dryhope (Driupp) Armstrong (mentioned in the Ballad of Kinmont Willie), also dwelt within its walls. With a Scott and an Armstrong as residents, it all proved too much for James VI, who in 1592 ordered Dryhope Pele to be demolished. Later it was rebuilt, but today it stands roofless and open, home only to the birds and vermin.

In 1784 an Italian balloonist "dropped in" to Dryhope Tower. Believing St Mary's Loch to be the North Sea he attempted an emergency landing, losing a flag, some rope and an anchor. Never ones to miss an opportunity, the Borderers cut up the flag for handkerchiefs.

(2) BLACKHOUSE. Yet another ancient pele tower, now totally ruined, the tower was built in the late 1600s. A Douglas stronghold, whose most famous son James Douglas, known as Black Douglas, cunningly captured Roxburgh Castle by disguising his forces as black oxen. Blackhouse Tower was the scene of the ballad so poignantly described in "The Douglas Tragedy". At the farm of Blackhouse James Hogg (the Ettrick Shepherd), was shepherd from 1790 to 1800, during which time he experienced the violent blizzard of 1794 (described by Hogg in *Blackwood's Magazine* of July 1819).

(3) DOUGLAS BURN. Legend has it that the stones high on the fell (now buried under a thick pall of Sitka Spruce), mark the site of the demise of Lady Margaret Douglas's seven brothers and her father, all of whom fell under the irresistible sword of her lover, who also perished in the dispute.

(4) "THE PLOVER'S WAILING CRY" - HOGG. For all its comic antics and synchronised flying displays the plover (or peewit) is not always a popular bird in the Borders. For it was the "wailing cry" of the plover when disturbed on these deserted fells that often led the Dragoons to the sorely persecuted Covenanters.

WALK 4. TIBBIE SHIELS INN - ST MARY'S LOCHSIDE - BOWERHOPE - ST MARY'S KIRK YARD - CAPPERCLEUCH - JAMES HOGG MONUMENT - TIBBIE SHIELS INN

St Mary's Loch, 3 miles long, is the largest and most picturesque loch in the Borderland. Crescent shaped and narrow, it nestles beneath steep sided hills, offering the hiker a walk of tranquility. Rich and varied in birdlife and plantlife, the walk around the lochside covers 7½ miles, with an ascent of less than 200 feet. It is graded 1 in difficulty, and can be enjoyed at a leisurely pace in 4 hours. Navigation and conditions underfoot do not present any problems, and in summer trainers can be worn. For those of you who value solitude, may I suggest a clear crisp day from December to March.

The loch lies alongside the A708 road 18 miles south-west of Selkirk, at the head of the fascinating Yarrow Valley. Car parking, *accommodation (including limited camping), and refreshments are all available at various establishments situated around the south end of the loch.*

Start the walk at Tibbie Shiels Inn (1), a quaint hotch-potch of white-washed buildings sheltered by a few trees of venerable age, on the southern tip of the loch. Walk though the car park and cross the stile, signposted "St Mary's Loch Sailing Club members only", to the lochside, passing in front of the sailing club-house. The trail soon reaches a path alongside the east bank of St Mary's Loch. This path, containing several stiles, is part of the Southern Upland Way, and as such is waymarked for the entire 3 miles, with the only habitation being the farm of Bowerhope (2), situated below the steep northern flank of Bowerhope Law 1,570 feet, some 2 miles from the starting point. The walk is a pleasant mix of old established coniferous and deciduous trees; not so the hillside above, which lies

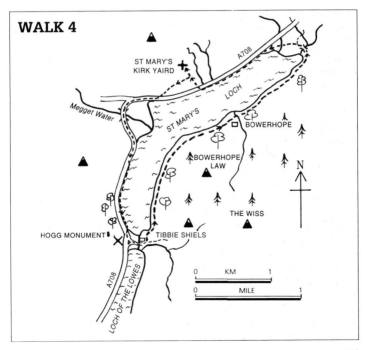

Monument to James Hogg, The Ettrick Shepherd

blanketed under acres of barely acceptable Sitka Spruce.

The northern end of the loch which feeds Yarrow Water is crossed by a bridge, leading north-west to the A708. At this point turn left to follow the shore-line west-south-west towards Cappercleuch. After approximately 1 mile, at GR 256235, leave the waterside to cross the road on the right to the sign 'St Mary's Kirkyard' (3). An interesting diversion, and a peaceful place from which to view the loch. The climb is sharp, but seats are thoughtfully provided. Return as far as the broad grassy track running through the bracken and parallel to the road, turn right and walk west on this quiet and scenic path until the road is reached. Care is needed until the village hall is passed and the wide and open bridge across Megget Water is crossed.

South from Megget bridge the route is shared with the internal combustion engine. There is, however, a wide grass verge and a shore-line that can be used, with exceptional views of the never ending charm of St Mary's Loch (4).

One and a half miles south of Megget bridge, overlooking the old bridge between the two lochs, stands a memorial to James Hogg, the Ettrick Shepherd (5). Visit the statue and read the verse. From this tribute to Hogg it is but a short step east over the narrow bridge to Tibbie Shiels.

Items of Interest Along the Way

(1) TIBBIE SHIELS INN. Tibbie's, that famous watering hole between St Mary's Loch and the Loch of the Lowes, so beloved by the literary giants of the last century, Scott, Hogg and North. Born in Ettrick in 1782, Tibbie Shiels lived in the cottage from 1823, with her husband Robert Richardson, a shepherd and mole catcher. Widowed the following year, this determined women turned the cottage into a welcoming haven for wayfarers who journeyed through the valleys of Yarrow and Moffat Water. The present bar, it is said, held thirteen small box-beds, rather like nocturnal coffins, and no doubt just as unhealthy!

(2) BOWERHOPE (pronounced Beer-op). The farmhouse kitchen in the early 1800s had such a low ceiling it caused the room to be perpetually full of smoke, yet farmer Sandy Cunningham is quoted as saying, "Ministers may talk o' Heevin' as they like; commend me to Bowerhope; I cud tak a tack (lease) o't to a' eternity." The present farmer breeds and rears Llamas, hiring the surplus males as pack animals to Southern Upland Wayfarers.

(3) ST MARY'S KIRK. Destroyed by fire in 1557 by a group of fractious Scotts, who unsuccessfully pursued a Cranston to the sanctuary within. It has never been rebuilt. The old kirk stood at the north-west corner of the present grave yard, and in memory of the Covenanters who often had only a blanket for shelter, a Blanket Preaching is held on the last Sunday each July. Seldom used today the Kirk Yard allows but a few privileged families of Brydon, Scott, Anderson, Armstrong and Grieve to rest within its stone walls.

(4) ST MARY'S LOCH.

> "What boon to lie, as I now lie,
> And see in silver at my feet
> Saint Mary's Lake, as if the sky
> Had fallen 'tween those hills so sweet."
> *Alexander Anderson*

(5) JAMES HOGG, THE ETTRICK SHEPHERD 1770-1835. Born at Ettrick Hall, a grand name for a rather damp little cottage (its walls fell down around 1830), Hogg is without doubt the greatest poet to spring from Border soil, and his fine memorial (by Andrew Currie, 1860) is placed above the junction of the lochs with the shepherd

151

holding a scroll in his left hand, "He taught the Wandering Winds to Sing."

> "Oft had he viewed, as morning rose,
> The Bosom of the Lonely Lowes:
> Oft thrilled his heart at close of even
> To see the dappled vales of heaven,
> With many a mountain moor and tree,
> Asleep upon Saint Mary."

WALK 5. TIBBIE SHIELS INN - LOCH OF THE LOWES - PEAT HILL - PIKESTONE RIG - PENIESTONE KNOWE - MID HILL - HERMAN LAW - BIRKHILL PASS - TIBBIE SHIELS INN

A loch side stroll followed by an exhilarating ridge walk around the corrie of Little Yarrow, allowing seldom seen views of the lochs of St Mary's and the Lowes. Nine and a half miles of varied grade 3 walking with 1,482 feet of ascent, and a journey time of 6 hours. The pathways vary from good grassy tracks and road side verges, to narrow sheep traces over the open fell. Walking boots and mountain clothing are recommended.

The walk commences by the historic inn of Tibbie Shiels, on the narrow isthmus between the lochs of St Mary and the Lowes, GR 241205 (services available). The A708 road linking Selkirk and Moffat runs along the shores of both lochs, and parking is available by the roadside between the lochs. From the road walk to the hump back bridge 100 yards from the inn, pass through the gate on the right that leads to the north end of the Loch of the Lowes.

A narrow path hugs the east side of the loch for its entire length of 1 mile. At the south end of the loch, prior to the farm of Riskinhope (1), turn left and leave the lochside to ascend the hillside on a narrow trace that rises with a deer fence. Follow the fence as it swings right to meet a broad and grassy farm track. This track is an alternative of the Southern Upland Way, and provides good walking south-east and then south for nearly 1 mile to Pikestone Rig 1,586 feet, with Peat Hill 1,508 feet on the left. At the col below Pikestone Rig, at GR 243175, leave the track for the open fell on the right, climbing steadily south-south-west for ³/₄ mile to Peniestone Knowe 1,807 feet.

Now high above the Southern Upland Way to Ettrick, our route joins a stone dyke running in from the left. This wall acts as a guide for the next $1^{1}/_{2}$ miles as it travels south-west for $^{1}/_{2}$ mile, then west for 1 mile through peat and poor paths, linking the Mid Hill watershed (2) to the 2,014 foot summit of Herman Law. In places this stretch can be somewhat glutinous underfoot, but the views to the north with the lochs far below more than compensate. From Herman Law the regional boundary fence runs west, descending steeply for $^{3}/_{4}$ mile to the road 900 feet below at Birkhill (3). With the fence on the right and a burn on the left the descent, though appearing steep, presents no problems, but do take care by the woodside should the grass be wet.

When the road is met at the cottage of Birkhill on the A708 turn right and follow the road north-east and then north for 3 miles to the south end of the Loch of the Lowes. The verges are wide and walkable, the scenery superb, and the motorists few and far between.

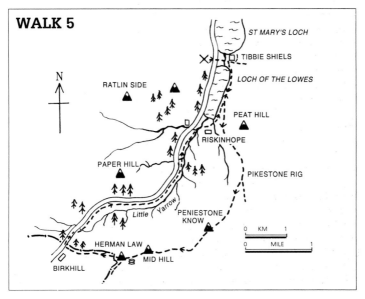

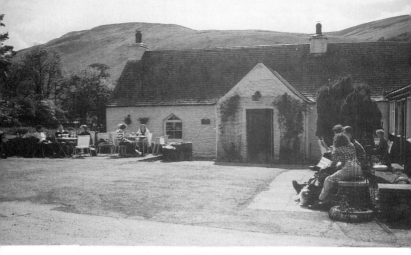

Tibbie Shiel's Inn

Before the loch is reached turn right at Chapelhope (4), onto the farm road to Riskinhope, from where the east side of the loch is reached, to rejoin the outward path and the last mile to Tibbie Shiels Inn.

Items of Interest Along the Way

(1) RISKINHOPE. It was at Riskinhope that Renwick, the last of the Scottish Covenanting martyrs preached and prayed with such fervour, that, according to the Ettrick Shepherd, "few of his hearers cheeks were dry". Renwick was executed at the Grassmarket in Edinburgh in February 1688.

(2) WATERSHED. Herman Law and Mid Hill are the northern tip of the watershed of the three valleys. To the north and the east the water drains into the Yarrow and the Ettrick, and thence into the Tweed and the North Sea. A matter of yards away, the water running south-west flows into Moffat Water, and eventually into the Irish Sea.

(3) BIRKHILL COTTAGE. Note the plaque on the wall to Mr Lapworth.

(4) CHAPELHOPE. Associated with James Hogg's rousing tale of Covenanting days, "Brownie of Bodesbeck".

WALK 6. TIBBIE SHIELS INN - SOUTHERN UPLAND WAY TO SCABCLEUCH - ETTRICK KIRK - PIKESTONE RIG - LOCH OF THE LOWES - TIBBIE SHIELS INN

An invigorating figure-of-eight fell walk, that encompasses two valleys, the Yarrow and the Ettrick. It includes a moorland ramble, and follows Scabcleuch Burn on its musical journey, to visit the birth place and the burial place of the Ettrick Shepherd. The 10½ mile adventure, with ascents of 1,550 feet is graded 3, and care is needed with navigation on the return journey (take a map and compass). The walk should be completed comfortably in 6½ hours.

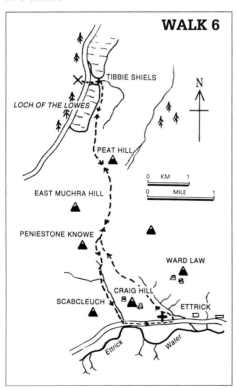

Car parking is available at the junction of the two lochs alongside the A708 road, GR 238205. With the James Hogg memorial directly behind, walk over the small stone bridge to the east and join the Southern Upland Way at Tibbie Shiels Inn (1).

Continue east past Crosscleuch, ascending steadily south-east along the farm road for approximately 1 mile. Here the Way leaves the broad track, turning right onto a narrow path (way-marked with the Thistle), through a plantation of rather

155

stunted conifers. The path, wet in places, is now quite distinct and well waymarked on its way south to the ruins of Riskinhope Hope (2). On the valley floor by the Whitehope Burn the path is somewhat wet and boggy underfoot, but once it climbs and contours south to below Peniestone Knowe 1,807 feet, conditions improve.

Continue south to the col ahead, from which the Ettrick Horseshoe (Walks 9, 9A, 9B) a semi-circle of 2,000 foot summits ringing Ettrick Head can be seen to the south west. Note also the gate with its signpost at the col, for this point is to be met on the return journey. The path now descends south-east, keep to the right of the two paths, waymarked with a thistle, and follow Scabcleuch Burn (a foul name for a fine burn) for 1 mile to the farm of Scabcleuch and a narrow metalled road.

Turn left at the road and leave the Southern Upland Way to meander eastwards for ³/₄ mile to the peace of Ettrick Kirk (3), surrounded by trees and guarded by constantly crowing rooks. To the west of the church by Craighill farm a signposted path 'St Mary's Loch' leads north west, rising steeply between Kirk Burn on the right and Craig Hill 1,597 feet on the left. Once the summit of Craig Hill is passed ³/₄ mile from Ettrick Kirk, the ground levels out, and the path dwindles to a narrow path. On a clear day the way can be distinguished quite easily by making directly for the summit of Peniestone Knowe (1 mile ahead to the north-west). In poor visibility the compass bearing is 310° magnetic for ¹/₂ hour over rough ground. Scabcleuch Burn needs to be crossed before the outward path is met by the signpost and the gate on Peniestone col.

Follow the outward path northwards to Pikestone Rig, turning left at the fork, to begin the long descent north-west on an ever widening grass track to the Loch of the Lowes. Take the narrow path along the east side of the loch to the old bridge by Tibbie Shiels Inn. *Accommodation and refreshments are available around the lochside of St Mary's.*

Items of Interest Along the Way

(1) TIBBIE SHIEL'S INN. When widowed in 1824, Isobella (Tibbie) Shiel, took in gentlemen lodgers to support herself and her six children, the first lodger being Robert Chalmers, researching his book *The Picture of Scotland*. A small active woman with an essential

sense of humour, Tibbie prophetically said, "Folk a' ken me best as Tibbie Shiels, and I dare say when I'm deid and gone this place will still be ca'ed Tibbie Shiels's." Today memorabilia from that bygone age decorate the inn, including a picture of Tibbie herself, complete with accompanying Ghost - seen only by those with the second sight, or those who have imbibed well but not too wisely!

(2) RISKINHOPE HOPE. Hope means a "sheltered valley", thus making this valley the valley above Riskinhope. Sadly, like so many of its kind in these high hills, the farm of Riskinhope Hope is but a grey and decaying ruin.

(3) ETTRICK KIRK. A new Kirk of Ettrick was built in the early sixteenth century, though the present church dates from 1824. A severe yet compelling building, it remains a "preaching kirk", with its pulpit and sounding board surmounted by a dove. The Kirk is closely linked to the unbending Calvanism of the Reverend Boston, "Boston of Ettrick", a minister whose hellfire sermons swelled the congregation from 57 in 1710, to 777 in 1731. From far and wide they came, no doubt on the same paths as are included in this guide.

In its churchyard lie the earthly remains of James Hogg, the Ettrick Shepherd, Tibbie Shiels who died in her 95th year, and William Laidlaw, whose headstone tells us "here lyeth William Laidlaw, the far famed Will of Phaup, who for feats of Frolic, Agility, and Strength, had no equal in his day." Will of Phaup was Hogg's grandfather, and the last man in Ettrick to speak to fairies.

Close by the Kirk, east towards the school stands another monument, commemorating the birth-place of the Ettrick Shepherd.

> "Where the pools are bright and deep,
> Where the grey trout lies asleep,
> Up the river and o'er the lea,
> That's the way for Billy and me".
>
> *"A Boy's Song", James Hogg*

WALK 7. TIBBIE SHIELS INN - CAPTAIN'S ROAD - THIRLSTANEHOPE - TUSHIELAW - NW ON B709 to GR 275201 - EARLS HILL - TIBBIE SHIELS INN

A circular walk from the Yarrow to the Ettrick and back, on a route often taken by Scott and Hogg, and much favoured by the Drovers. No navigational problems, on good paths and roads, this grade 2 walk will be completed within 7 hours. Good conditions underfoot, coupled with the even spread of the 1,660 foot ascent, make this 12 mile walk seem much shorter than it actually is.

Park the car on the verge of the A708 road, where the Loch of the Lowes and St Mary's Loch are joined by a narrow neck of land. At the entrance to Tibbie Shiels Inn the road is signposted "Southern Upland Way", follow this road east past Crosscleuch, as it climbs south-east to the north side of Earl's Hill. At this point a directional post "Public footpath to Hopehouse by the Captain's Road", indicates a split in the route. Take the indicated "Captain's Road" (1) on the

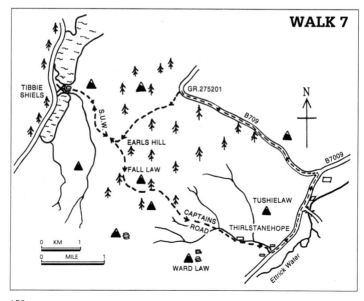

Tibbie Shiel's and Ox Cleuch Rig

path to the south east, as far as another signpost "Captain's Road - Ettrick and Tushielaw". Veer to the left as the path winds and twists around the tree clad flanks of Fall Law 1,828 feet and Cowan's Croft 1,897 feet, ascending and descending south-east for 3½ miles to the Ettrick Valley. Once Cowan's Croft is passed, the descending path past Shepherdscleuch Cairn and Hopehouse Burn winding down to Thirlstanehope is particularly pleasing.

At the B709 road at Wardlaw turn left, Thirlestane Tower (2) lies 1 mile to the right, and note the milestones on this road which appear every ½ mile! Follow the road for nearly 2 miles to the junction of Tushielaw (3), a scenically pleasing road passing an ancient pele tower and the sloping bridge straddling Ettrick Water by Tushielaw Inn, a suggested refreshment stop.

Once the road junction by Tushielaw Farm is reached take the left fork west, and then north-west along a narrow minor road for 3 miles to GR 275201. The climb is gradual and there is much that pleases the eye en route. At GR 275201 swing left onto a forest track, signposted "vehicles at drivers own risk", to walk west and then south-west for 1½ miles and eventually join the outgoing "Captain's Road", and return to Tibbie Shiels Inn. *Refreshments and*

159

accommodation are available at the start, the halfway point and the finish of the walk.

Items of Interest Along the Way

(1) CAPTAIN'S ROAD. Thomson's map of Selkirkshire 1824, lists the "Captains Road" from St Mary's Loch to Tushielaw as a drove road, linking it into the chain of drove roads running south from Peebles, through the glen of the Douglas Burn and Dryhope (Walk 3) via St Mary's Loch (Walk 4), and south from Tushielaw alongside the Rankle Burn to the valley of the Teviot at Hawick.

(2) THIRLESTANE TOWER. A ruin today, cut to stubble height by the severe arm of the Earl of Hertford as he slashed his infamous swath through the Borders in 1544 and 1545. The pele tower belonged then to Sir John Scott, whose descendant Lord Napier of Ettrick (motto "Readdy, ay Readdy") has his seat in nearby Thirlestane, a mansion built in the early 1800s.

(3) TUSHIELAW. Also has its ruined pele tower, this one being the stronghold of Adam Scott of Tushielaw, King of the Thieves. Folklore has it that Adam was hanged from a branch of his own ash tree within his tower's walls. Facts never quite make such a good story; he was executed in 1530 in Edinburgh for taking Blackmail. Reivers, such as Adam Scott perfected the protection racket, spawning the word "blackmail".

WALK 8. BIRKHILL - MID RIG - ANDREWHINNEY HILL - BODESBECK LAW - GR 173096 - BUSHIE LAW - BELL CRAIG - TROWGRAIN MIDDLE - HERMAN LAW - BIRKHILL

Choose a day when the cloud is high and the air is clear for this walk along the ridge of Bodesbeck, high above the glaciated U-shaped valley of Moffat Water. This is a classic walk of its kind, justly graded 3, the 12 miles include six summits of 2,000 feet plus, though once height is attained there are no severe ascents on the ridge. The total ascent for the journey is 2,276 feet, and walking time should be in the region of 7½ hours. Paths and tracks are mostly distinct and good underfoot, though it is recommended boots,

Dob's Linn Gorge and Birkhill Pass (Walk 4.1)
A Standing Stone and the Warriors Rest (Walk 3.2)

Ice in Midlaw Burn Gorge (Walk 4.2a)

Days past in Gameshope (Walk 4.5)

adequate clothing, a map and compass, together with food and drink, be taken. Do not forget the camera and a spare roll of film.

Birkhill (1), a lonely roadside cottage 1,108 feet above sea level, at GR 202159 on the A708 road 22 miles south-west of Selkirk, marks the start of the walk. Parking is limited to a small lay-by in the plantation 200 yards north of Birkhill. A distinct and steep path is clearly visible to the south, ascending across the western flank of Trowgrain Middle 2,058 feet. Ascend with the path for 1 mile, crossing Raking Gill, until the ridge joining Herman Law and Andrewhinney Hill is met at 2,114 feet. This ridge is clearly marked by the fence/stone dyke of the regional boundary, its ascent and the subsequent walk to Andrewhinney Hill (2) 2,221 feet, offer exciting glimpses west over the Moffat Water Valley and Birkhill Pass to

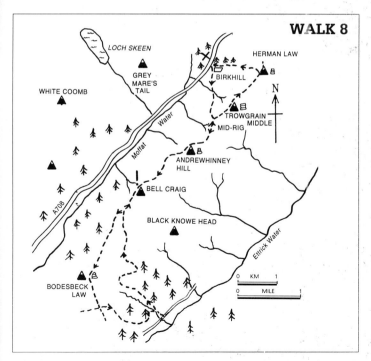

Dob's Linn Gorge, the Grey Mare's Tail, Loch Skeen, and White Coomb 2,696 feet (Chapter 4, Walks 1, 2, 2A, 3).

At 2,221 feet Andrewhinney Hill (2) is the highest point on the 3 mile ridge walk to Bodesbeck Law 2,173 feet. The faint path continues south-south-west in a somewhat haphazard fashion, rising and falling according to the whim of each summit. With Moffat Water 1,500 feet below, the summits of Bell Craig 2,047 feet, (with its rocky outcrops and severe drops), and Mid Rig 2,018 feet, are all too soon passed to reach the fine grandstand of Bodesbeck Law (3) 2,173 feet, an ideal spot to rest and enjoy a break. The steep descent south from Bodesbeck Law follows the stone dyke of the regional boundary to the col below, meeting a bridlepath from the Ettrick Valley. At this point turn left, to descend east between various coniferous plantations. The track forks twice; always take the left hand fork until the trail ends at Longhope Burn. Cross the burn and immediately turn left, onto another forest road ascending north-west over Bushie Law to Bught Hill. From Bught Hill traverse the open fell north for 1 mile to the boundary wall of the outward journey, south of Bell Craig.

From Bell Craig be guided north by the stone dyke/fence for $2^3/4$ miles to the summit of Herman Law 2,014 feet, passing Trowgrain Middle 2,058 feet on the way. These two summits, crowned with well constructed angular cairns (rarely seen on these hills), were not walked on the outward journey. At Herman Law the boundary fence swings sharply west, ie. left, and descends steeply. Care is needed by the woodside as the way is steep, and in wet conditions slippery underfoot. At the base of the plantation it's a short and easy step to the cottage of Birkhill. *The nearest accommodation and refreshments are at St Mary's Loch.*

Items of Interest Along the Way

(1) BIRKHILL. A solitary and lonely cottage by the roadside of the A708 near the summit of Birkhill Pass 1,108 feet, considered by many to be the finest Border pass of all. The cottage carries a plaque "Birkhill Cottage, where between 1872 and 1877 Charles Lapworth recognised the value of Graptolites, as a clue to the geological structure of these hills. Erected by Scottish Geologists in 1951".

(2) ANDREWHINNEY HILL 2,220 feet. A fine vantage point from which to appreciate the views, and scotch the rumour that all that is south of the Highlands is flat. For not only do the Southern Uplands qualify in height as mountains, they also qualify in certain areas as perfect examples of the mountain form, small in size but beautifully proportioned.

(3) BODESBECK LAW 2,173 feet. Stands guard over Bodesbeck farm, as in Hogg's "Brownie of Bodesbeck". To the north and north-west, the deep and dramatic Blackhope Glen lies imprisoned by Saddle Yoke 2,413 feet, Saddle Craigs, Hart Fell 2,651 feet, and Swatte Fell 2,389 feet (Chapter 4, Walk 4). To the south-west the narrow glen of Moffat Water unfolds with a patchwork of in-bye fields as the town of Moffat is approached, and below the occasional "Dinkey toy" crawls ant-like along the hair line of the road. South and east the Ettrick Water gathers strength as it breaks free from the three sided grip of the Ettrick Horseshoe, White Shank 2,035 feet, Capel Fell 2,223 feet, Wind Fell 2,180 feet, and Ettrick Pen 2,270 feet (Walks 9, 9A, 9B).

WALK 9. POTBURN GR 188093 - BODESBECK COL - WHITE SHANK - CAPEL FELL - ETTRICK HEAD - WIND FELL - HOPETOUN CRAIG - ETTRICK PEN - OVER PHAWHOPE - POTBURN GR 188093

Not a journey to be undertaken during winter's icy grip, but when the sun is warm on the back, and the winds have lost their thinness, then is the time to tackle and enjoy the Ettrick Horseshoe. Ten miles of high level walking at its best, covering six summits of 2,000 feet. Graded 3, with a total ascent of 2,265 feet (in places steep but never hazardous), the circular walk can be completed in 6 exhilarating hours. Paths at the lower levels are good and distinct, but on the heights they are little more than sheep traces, and in some stretches non-existent. However navigation is simplified by the boundary dyke/fence that runs for the entire length of the Horseshoe. Boots and correct clothing are essential, and a map and compass are recommended, together with a camera to record the solitude of these lonely domed mountains.

The 24 mile drive from Selkirk along the banks of Ettrick Water is a pleasant experience, especially in spring and autumn. First on the B7009, Selkirk to Tushielaw (accommodation and food for Walks 9, 9A and 9B), then the B709 road to Ramseycleuch, where a narrow road with passing places, signposted Ettrick, forks to the right. Follow this road west and south-west for 7 miles, to the end of the public road at South Potburn GR 188093. Parking is available on the edge of the turning circle.

From the starting point of the walk at GR 188093, 1,200 feet above sea level, an unbroken horseshoe of mountains rises high above the coniferous tide mark, an indication that this promises to be a walk of the highest quality. Pass through the right hand gate onto the forest road leading west; after several hundred yards fork left to ford Longhope Burn onto a grassy path running between the trees. Walk south-west and then west climbing steadily, passing two gates and a circular sheep stell (keep to the right at the fork).

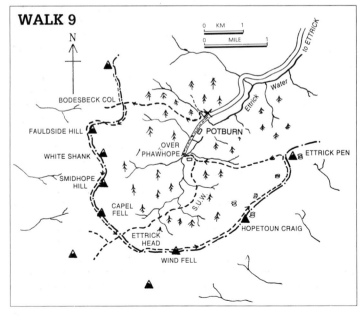

Bodesbeck col 1,555 feet, with its dilapidated gate at the regional boundary is reached after 40 minutes. To the right the summit of Bodesbeck Law, to the left White Shank.

Leave the path at the col and follow the stone dyke left, ie. south, to the immediate skyline, from where it zig-zags west across a pathless waste, later to swing left, ie. south, at the summit of Fauldside Hill 1,858 feet, before rising steadily to White Shank 2,035 feet. Do not at any point on this walk doubt the accuracy of the boundary wall/fence as your guide, keep it in sight and to hand all the way to Ettrick Pen 2,270 feet. During the ascent of White Shank, which should be reached 1¹/₂ hours from the start, stop and look west across the Moffat Water Valley to the exciting prospect of rock in the dramatic glen of Blackhope (Chapter 4, Walk 4). The way from White Shank over Capel Fell to Ettrick Head, though somewhat of a switch-back, is never dull. First Smidhope Hill 2,111 feet, the guiding wall is replaced by a fence that swings left to the summit. At the gate on the summit descend with the fence to the left, ie. south-east, to Ettrick Head 1,700 feet. This stretch is perhaps the wildest and most desolate of the walk, with deep and dark ravines scouring the rounded hillsides to the south, and ahead a black mass of peat loitering with intent at the foot of the steep sided Wind Fell 2,180 feet.

The Southern Upland Way intersects the route at Ettrick Head with the heartening notice "Welcome to Borders Region", prominently displayed. Ahead the ascent of Wind Fell 2,180 feet requires some determination due to the absence of paths and the initial crossing of the peat, but once attained it marks the start of another fine ridge walk. Continue north-east for nearly 2 miles over Hopetoun Craig 2,075 feet to Ettrick Pen at 2,270 feet, the highest point on the walk. This section offers fine views on all sides, particularly south to Eskdalemuir. The approaches to Ettrick Pen are marked by a clutch of well constructed cairns, though the summit cairn is somewhat untidy.

Leave the summit cairn and the guiding fence for an adventurous hike of over ¹/₂ mile, descending the open fell of Ettrick Pen's west ridge. On a clear day the line of descent is towards the summit of White Shank, 2 miles to the west. In poor visibility descend on a compass bearing of 282° magnetic. The ridge and the shoulder are not difficult to negotiate, and the marker to aim for is an old tin shed by the Entertrona Burn. From the tin shed descend to the valley floor and the "bothy" at Over Phawhope (a bed for the night if required).

The Southern Upland Way is met at the bothy and followed across the wooden bridge via Potburn to the turning point on the public road, GR 188093. *A campsite is situated between Ettrick Village and Tushielaw (inn accommodation and refreshment) on the B709 road, B&Bs are also sprinkled along Ettrick Valley for all number 9 walks.*

WALK 9A. POTBURN GR 188093 - OVER PHAWHOPE - ETTRICK HEAD - WIND FELL - ETTRICK PEN - OVER PHAWHOPE - POTBURN GR 188093

This variation of Walk 9, enables the walker to sample a valley walk to the watershed at Ettrick Head, yet still accomplish the exhilaration and the

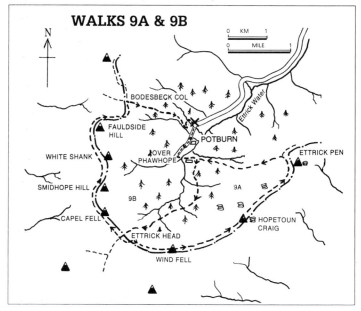

166

visual pleasure of the high ridge by walking one half of the Ettrick Horseshoe. Graded 2, the distance is 6 miles, with a total ascent of 1,170 feet. Conditions underfoot for this 4 hour hike are mainly along farm/forest roads, with 2¹/₂ miles on the open fell. Visually pleasing and very photogenic, with a high interest factor.

From the turning point at GR 188093, take the wide farm road south to South Potburn, clearly visible ahead. Continue to follow the road to the wooden bridge and the bothy of Over Phawhope. A few yards past the bothy, the road swings right at the Entertrona Burn and continues south along the valley for 1¹/₄ miles to Ettrick Head. On all sides coniferous plantations mask the rolling hillsides, though clearings have been left by the banks of Ettrick Water. Once clear of these sterile woodlands the path to Ettrick Head on the Regional Boundary is distinct and most welcome.

Over the stile and sharp left, first circumnavigate the deep peat, and then ascend the steep flank of Wind Fell 2,180 feet, using the ever present boundary fence as a guide. The ridge walk north-east from the summit of Wind Hill via the craggy top of Hopetoun Craig 2,075 feet, to the majestic cairn on Ettrick Pen 2,270 feet, is 2 miles of pedestrian pleasure. Keep an eye open for the fine selection of cairns on the approach to Ettrick Pen.

Leave the large cairn and make for the trackless open fell due west, use the peak of White Shank, 2 miles across the Ettrick Valley, as a marker and in poor visibility, a bearing of 282° magnetic. Descend the western ridge to a tin hut on the Entertrona Burn where a good wide track is met. This pathway descends sedately west to Over Phawhope bothy, an opportunity for a break and a look at the visitors' book before returning north on the farm road to Potburn, and the starting point.

WALK 9B. POTBURN GR 188093 - OVER PHAWHOPE - ETTRICK HEAD - CAPEL FELL - WHITE SHANK - BODESBECK COL - POTBURN GR 188093

This walk is for the enthusiast who for various reasons has limited time or energy at his/her disposal, but who nevertheless has the urge to go just that little bit further. This tempting aperitif is graded 2, with an overall ascent of 1,123 feet in the 7 mile journey, which can be completed in 4 hours. Conditions underfoot are good, walking boots are nevertheless recommended. Take a map, if only to identify the tempting bits west of Moffat Water.

Start the ramble at GR 188093, and take the route to the stile at Ettrick Head as described in Walk 9A. At the regional boundary, having crossed the stile, do not immediately turn right and leave the Southern Upland Way but continue south for ¹/₂ mile to gaze into the jaws of Selcoth Burn on the southern flanks of Capel Fell. Retrace your steps to the stile, turn left to follow the fence as it climbs 520 feet, to the summit of Capel Fell 2,223 feet.

On the flat and pleasant summit, once past the gate and alongside the right hand fence, the views to the west and north will commence to tease and excite for the next 2 miles north. Follow the fence/stone dyke, first over the narrow col from Capel Fell to Smidhope Hill 2,111 feet, admiring the corries and gullies to the east and west, then stroll to White Shank to gaze at the rocky crags of Saddle Craigs and Swatte Fell to the west across the Moffat Water Valley. Use the wall and fence as an aid to navigation on the winding descent via Fauldside Hill, 1,858 feet, to the rickety gate on Bodesbeck Col.

The gate on the col straddles the path from the Ettrick Valley, so turn right and descend east through two gates, keeping to the left forks at any dividing of the ways. The path enters another collection of conifers and ends abruptly at Longhope Burn, ford the burn to join another wide forest road to the right. One more gate and 300 yards returns the walker to the starting point at GR 188093.

WALK 10. ETTRICKBRIDGE - HOWFORD HILL - HELMBURN HILL - ETTRICKBRIDGE WOODEND - KIRKHOPE TOWER - KIRKHOPE - ETTRICKBRIDGE

A figure-of-eight walk, winding through the broad lower reaches of Ettrick Water, this low level walk is equally appealing in the fresh green of spring or later when the woods and hedgerows are splashed with nature's fiery palette. The pathways are good on this grade 1 walk of 6¹/₂ miles, the ascent of 490 feet negligible, and the two loops from the hamlet of Ettrickbridge can be completed in 3½ hours walking time.

Ettrickbridge (1) nestles on Ettrick Water some 7 miles along the B7009 road south-west of Selkirk. Parking can be had in the village, but please take care not to block access. The village inn on the north side of the main street provides a natural starting and finishing point for the walk. From the inn walk east to cross the bridge (1), and follow the road east for 700 yards; at the small copse on the left turn right. Follow the farm road left to wind south-east. After ½ mile the road forks, take the left track and contour with the road as it turns south past three plantations.

At the third plantation the road becomes a bridleway, which after 400 yards forks. Travel via the right fork and loop north-west below Helmburn Hill, returning after 1 mile via Helmburn to Ettrickbridge. Turn left and cross the bridge; once across Ettrick Water turn sharp right and follow the road past the church to Woodend and the cemetery.

With the cemetery on the left, follow the bridlepath north-west for ¾ mile to the distinct and well preserved pele tower of Kirkhope

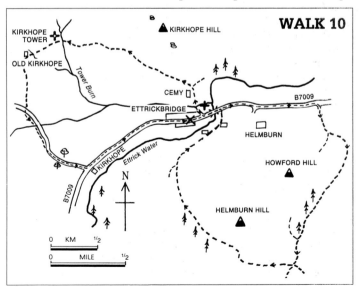

(2), and the picturesque Kirkhope Linns. From the tower walk east to Kirkhope and join the farm road south to the cattle grid and thence to the farm of Kirkhope on the B7009. At Kirkhope turn left, returning to Ettrickbridge ¹/₂ mile to the north-east.

Refreshment and accommodation are available in the village, and the walk can be split into two, with a break in this charming Ettrick hamlet.

Items of Interest Along the Way

(1) ETTRICKBRIDGE. Known also as Ettrickbridgend in older books, and named as such on old maps, this quiet hamlet straddles the now substantial water of Ettrick as it flows north-east to join the Tweed at Selkirk. It is said that the first bridge to span Ettrick Water was built by "Auld Wat Scott of Harden", a little way above the present bridge. A stone from Wat's bridge, bearing the Harden coat of arms, is embedded in the present structure.

(2) KIRKHOPE TOWER. Now in an unstable state, this pele tower was once home to that notorious freebooter Auld Wat of Harden, the same Wat who built the bridge at Ettrickbridge. Tradition has it that Wat built it to salve his conscience, after a boy kidnapped by him had drowned when attempting to cross the ford.

Chapter 4: The Tweedsmuir Hills

THE AREA

Within the environs of the Tweedsmuir Hills lie two distinctive groups of mountains, the Moffat Hills and the Manor Hills, which between them form the western bastion to the Scottish Border country covered in this guide.

The Moffat Hills. Neatly enclosed in a triangle of rivers and roads, these fascinating hills offer an impressively compelling landscape, particularly when viewed from the A708 road that winds through the Moffat Water Valley. It is from this steep sided glen that the wild lateral valleys of Blackhope, Carrifran, and the Grey Mare's Tail (Walks 1, 2, 2A, 3 and 4) curve gracefully and seductively northwards, offering an enticing invitation to the walker. These glaciated intrusions, penetrating deeply into the central plateau, are ringed by spectacular stretches of broken rocky crags, loose shale and scree, and divided by sharp and narrow grassy ridges. Steep cliffs and boulder strewn slopes in excess of 1,000 feet emphasise the plunging nature of the south-eastern section of these hills.

In addition to the glaciated glens the Moffat Hills contain gorges and gullies, some exposed for all to see, the more interesting remaining hidden in dark and secretive hillsides. Two lochs, Loch Skeen 1,700 feet and Gameshope Loch 1,850 feet, dwell high in the range, whilst at lower levels the narrow reservoirs of Talla and Megget securely lock the northern boundaries of the group.

Contained in the Moffat Hills are four mountains over 2,500 feet - White Coomb, Hart Fell, Lochcraig Head and Molls Cleuch Dod - together with two tops that exceed that height, Firthope Rig and Great Hill. There are six hills over 2,000 feet - Under Saddle Yoke, Swatte Fell, Cape Law, Garelet Dod, Erie Hill and Whitehope Heights, and nine tops - Nickies Knowe, Carrifran Gans, Saddle Yoke, Carlavin Hill, Nether Coomb Craig, Falcon Craig, Lairds Cleuch Rig, Garelet Hill and Din Law.

This isolated and lonely area is so devoid of human habitation that not one road or farm track entering these hills completes its journey to emerge at the other side. The few isolated hill farms that inhabit the hills can only be found on the extremities. The landscape of the Tweedsmuir Hills is rich in wild life: ravens, ring ouzels and red grouse inhabit the higher fells while herons, dippers, grey wagtails and sand pipers favour Moffat Water and the lower burns. Feral goats, fox, otters, feral mink, mountain hares and the occasional deer can all be found. Limestone loving plants are present at lower levels, whilst the upper ground is covered by the acid loving plants such as heaths and heather. On wet and badly drained cols, ubiquitous peat hags lurk, with half hidden wet holes innocently covered by bright green featherbed moss. The roads ringing the area are the A708 St Mary's Loch to Moffat, the A701 Moffat to Tweedsmuir, and the unclassified road running from Tweedsmuir via Talla and Megget reservoirs to St Mary's Loch.

The Manor Hills. Rising north of the Moffat Hills these hills are wild and exposed on their eastern and southern flanks, though this severity is tempered on the west and north by the unmistakable beauty of the Upper Tweed Valley, the intriguing Manor Water Valley, and that of Quair Water. The range consists of an upland sprawl of lumpy rounded grassy summits joined together by broad ridges that run willy-nilly over the entire plateau. Lacking the form and character of the more dramatic Moffat Hills they have one great virtue, gentle slopes. With dry conditions underfoot and the assistance of boundary fences/dykes to aid navigation the miles can be traversed with some ease and not a little aplomb. The main ridge runs north from Cramalt Craig to flank and overlook the nine miles of Manor Valley, whilst the more shapely ridges of the massif descend in graceful curves to the Tweed between Drumelzier (pronounced (Drum-eelier) and Cademuir Hill, south of Peebles.

If height is an attraction, this massif contains some of the highest mountains in southern Scotland, and certainly the highest in the Border Region. There are two mountains over 2,700 feet, Broad Law and Cramalt Craig, with one over 2,600 feet, Dollar Law, and one top, Fifescar Knowe. Ten hills exceed 2,000 feet - Dun Rig, Pykestone Hill, Glenrath Heights, Middle Hill, Black Law, Talla Cleuch Head, Stob Law, Drumezlier Law, Birkscairn Hill and Greenside Law, with six tops in excess of 2,000 feet - The Scrape, Blackhouse Heights, Clockmore, Hunt Law, Taberon Law, and Deer Law.

Lochs and rocks are minimal, Loch Eddy being the only stretch of water of any note, though the southern boundary is restrained by St Mary's Loch and the man-made reservoirs of Megget and Talla. Rock and scree can be found at Polmood Craig on the north face of Broad Law, the small but picturesque Bitch Craig at Manorhead, and also at Juniper Craig below Preston Law.

The Manor Hills are encircled by roads, the A701 Tweedsmuir to Drumelzier, the B712 to Peebles and the A72 to Innerleithen, where a right turn onto the B709 travels south to join the A708 to St Mary's Loch, with an unclassified single track road leading west via the reservoirs of Megget and Talla to Tweedsmuir.

Peebles, Innerleithen, Moffat and Selkirk provide the widest variety of accommodation for the Tweedsmuir Hills, ranging from hotels to camp/caravan sites. Inns and small hotels are found at St Mary's Loch, Tweedsmuir and Mountbenger, with a selection of bed and breakfasts scattered along the roads surrounding the hills. Scotland's first youth hostel is situated at Broadmeadows, 4 miles west of Selkirk.

Public bus services are none too frequent. Details can be obtained at the bus stations in Peebles, Innerleithen and Selkirk, and from the local tourist information centres. Post buses run to the more remote regions, invariably early in the day.

Donald's Cleuch Head

THE WALKS

Maps recommended: OS Landranger 1:50,000, Sheets 72, 73, 78 and 79.

With not one Munro in the area the hills are not bagged to death by the relentless tramp of "tickers" feet, and as a result the seekers of solitude can find just that. Walk 1 visits two fine waterfalls, in addition to introducing the walker to this spectacular upland area. Walk 2 climbs past the thundering falls of the Grey Mare's Tail to venture onto the high plateau, giving a bird's eye view of Loch Skeen, the black loch 1,700 feet above sea level. For the more adventurous Walk 2A includes all the pleasures of Walk 2, but adds a steep scramble in the narrow confines of Midlaw Burn Gorge. Continuing in the energetic mood Walk 3 treks into Carrifran glen below the dramatic face of Raven Craig, ascending to the highest summit in the Moffat Hills, White Coomb. Having sighted the graceful narrow curving ridge of Saddle Yoke from Carrifran Gans, Walk 4 will have become imprinted on the walker's mind. The high level circuit of the wild and precipitous Blackhope Glen over Saddle Yoke, Hart Fell and Swatte Fell is in my opinion the finest of Border journeys. Walk 5's entry into the Moffat Hills is from the northern extremity of the range, via the mysterious glen of Gameshope, to a ridge carrying four 2,500 foot mountains.

Walks 6 and 6A introduce the Manor Hills, by ascending the gentle slopes of the highest mountain in the range, Broad Law 2,754 feet, with Walk 6A including the second highest, Cramalt Craig 2,723 feet. The ascent of both is cushioned by starting the walk from 1,483 feet, the same height and starting point as Walk 7, which romps over the north ridge of the photogenic Talla valley returning alongside the reservoir to finish by Talla Linn. Walk 8 starts in Manor Water Glen at Langhaugh, ascending alongside Kirkhope Burn to stride over Newholm Hill, Long Grain Knowe, Pykestone Hill and finish on the eyrie of Posso Craig. Walk 9 is through the delightful glen of Quair Water, with the secluded Loch Eddy at its head, then over the heather clad hills of Blake Muir. Finally Walk 10 clips the extreme eastern tip of the Manor foothills, over the fine open ridges of Broomy Law and the Three Brethren, descending to the picturesque Tweed.

INFORMATION TABLE

WALK	DISTANCE/ MILES	ASCENT	DEGREE OF DIFFICULTY*	TIME/ HOURS
1	4	1,000ft	3	3/3½
2	7	2,024ft	3	5
2A	7	2,154ft	4	6
3	7	2,355ft	4	5
4	10	2,445ft	4	5/7
5	8	1,700ft	3	5
6	6	1,320ft	2	3½
6A	9	1,970ft	3	5
7	8	1,415ft	3	5
8	6½	1,654ft	3	4
9	10	1,450ft	2	5½
10	7½	1,123ft	2	5

*DEGREE OF DIFFICULTY

1 - Good path, moderate ascent, no navigational problems.
2 - Distinct path, steeper ascents, longer walk.
3 - Paths rough in places, ascent 2,000 feet, exposed in places.
4 - Few paths, ascent 2,400 feet plus, exposed, compass needed.

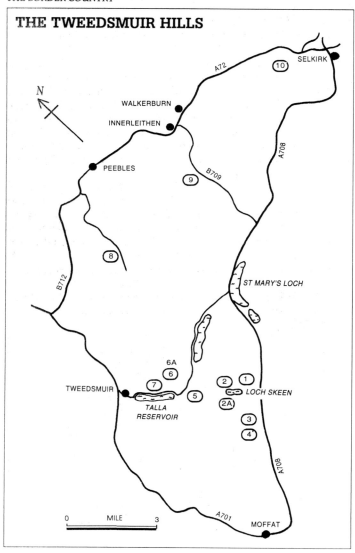

THE **TWEEDSMUIR HILLS**

N

A72

⑩ SELKIRK

WALKERBURN

INNERLEITHEN

A708

B709

PEEBLES

⑨

B712

⑧

ST MARY'S LOCH

6A
⑥

TWEEDSMUIR

⑦

⑤

② ①
⑳ LOCH SKEEN
②A

③
④'

TALLA
RESERVOIR

A708

A701

0   MILE   3

MOFFAT

WALK 1. GREY MARE'S TAIL - TAIL BURN - BRAN LAW - WATCH KNOWE - DOB'S LINN - GREY MARE'S TAIL

Situated barely 1 mile apart, the cascades of the Grey Mare's Tail (1) and Dob's Linn (3) differ vastly in appearance. This circular walk embraces both waterfalls, and introduces the walker to the classic glaciated valley of Moffat Water (2) and the Moffat Hills. A relatively short walk of 4 miles, with a total ascent of 1,000 feet, it is graded 3 (the descent into the gorge of Dob's Linn involves a scramble over wet rocks and loose shale). The walk should be completed in 3 to 3½ hours. Walking boots with good gripping soles are essential, and if photography is of interest the morning light is the best.

The walk starts from the A708 road, 24 miles south-west of Selkirk, and 10 miles north-east of Moffat. Adequate free car parking is available on both sides of the road at GR 187145. A stepped path leads from the car park, with the way glued onto the steep hillside ascending on the right for nearly ¾ mile (do not abandon the path as some sections are quite exposed). When the Grey Mare's Tail (1) is passed and the ascent flattens out turn sharp right, ie. east, to leave the path and climb to the shoulder of Bran Law. There are no immediate paths over this open fell, but soon a distinct sheep trace

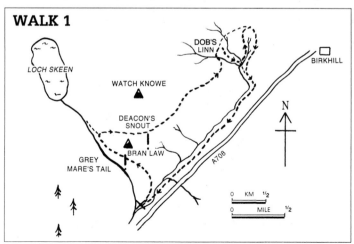

is joined as it contours east, and then north-east, around the rim of Bran Law quaintly and accurately known as Deacon's Snout. Care is needed as the exposure to the right is severe, though the views of the glen of Moffat Water (2) are most rewarding. From the rocky rim contour north below Watch Knowe for ³/₄ mile, passing above three narrow gullies which run steeply down to the road below.

The multiple and severe gullies of Dob's Linn (3) appear unexpectedly, the first gully has a sizeable burn running into it (feeding Dob's Linn), with a few stunted trees clinging precariously to the sheer rim. ON NO ACCOUNT must a descent be attempted into this gully. Circle north above the head of the waterfall to a second gully opening to the right, with one small burn trickling into it from the open fell, GR 195159. This cleuch can be descended with care by entering from a point by a solitary tree halfway between the two burns, and traversing the grassy slope to the north burn. Once this burn is reached descend carefully alongside the wet rocks, utilising a faint goat trace, until the sheer gully carrying Dob's Linn is joined on the right. The five falls and slides of Dob's Linn are now in full view. The path to the valley floor is distinct, and when the lower levels are reached turn left to explore the third and largest of the gullies. The ascent of this very narrow gorge necessitates frequent crossings of the burn, and care is needed in the upper reaches when scrambling over the crumbling and unstable shale.

Not only are the rocks and plants in these gullies of interest (3), but also be on the lookout for a herd of feral goats. Emerging from the head of the last gully turn right to the fence, pass through the gate and descend south with the fence to the mouth of the gorge. The walk to the car park is a pleasant 1¼ miles south-west in Birkhill Pass alongside the infant Moffat Water. *Rest and refreshments can be had at various establishments around St Mary's Loch.*

Items of Interest Along the Way

(1) GREY MARE'S TAIL. This spectacular waterfall, with its 200 foot drop, falls through one of the most striking examples of a hanging valley in the south of Scotland. During the Ice Age a large glacier gouged a much deeper channel into the Moffat Water Valley than did the smaller side glaciers, forming a step that left the resultant Tail Burn hanging; it took the route of least resistance,

hence the eye-catching Grey Mare's Tail.

(2) MOFFAT WATER GLEN. When ice covered the country, a main and swiftly moving glacier gouged out what is now the Moffat Water glen, and was fed by smaller lateral glaciers. Large quantities of sand, clay and rocks were dumped at the side of the main glen and in the side valleys, and these "Kames" can be seen today as vegetation covered mounds.

(3) DOB'S LINN. Whilst not as awesome as the Grey Mare's Tail, the five falls and water slides of Dob's Linn are just as dramatic and in some ways more picturesque, as they slide down the exposed face of two sheer slabs of rock. The geologist Charles Lapworth contributed greatly to our understanding of geological time, with his work around Dob's Linn. He made a special study of fossilised "Graptolites", small plankton eating animals that lived some 300 million years ago on the surface of ancient seas, their remains becoming incorporated in the sediments of these seas to produce the sandstones and shales from which the present day landscape was formed.

WALK 2. GREY MARE'S TAIL (CAR PARK) - TAIL BURN - LOCH SKEEN - LOCHCRAIG HEAD - FIRTHYBRIG HEAD - FIRTHY-BRIG RIG - RIDGE WEST OF LOCH SKEEN - GREY MARE'S TAIL (CAR PARK)

A steeply ascending path leads the walker above the spectacular falls of the Grey Mare's Tail to begin an elevated circuit of the dark and rather secretive loch, Loch Skeen. Graded 3, the 7 mile walk contains a total ascent of 2,024 feet, on steep pathways and grassy tracks. Exhilarating but never hazardous, the walk will take 5 hours at the most. Mountain walking footwear and clothing are needed, and in adverse weather a map and compass are essential.

The A708, Moffat to Selkirk road, has several car parks at the roadside below the falls of the Grey Mare's Tail, at GR 187145. From the car park (very popular in summer with coach trips), take the stepped path to climb steeply up the flank of Bran Law north of the Grey Mare's Tail (1). Above the falls the path winds north-west alongside Tail Burn, through a rather desolate area of glacial pimples, to the foot of Loch Skeen (2). Before the loch, at the point where Midlaw Burn runs into the Tail Burn from the left, a faint and narrow trace through the heather leaves the main path on the right to ascend over a glacial mound. Take this heathery trace north for ¹/₂ mile, to the angle in the fence leading north to Lochcraig Head.

Loch Skeen is now several hundred yards to the west, ie. left, with the steep face of Lochcraig Head a cruel mix of bare rock and sheer scree to the north. Further west a stark ridge from Firthybrig Head combines to give the loch its reputation as "a gloomy tarn". On reaching the fence turn left and follow the path north for 1 mile, ascending steeply for 800 feet to the flat glassy summit of Lochcraig Head (3) 2,625 feet, the zenith of the walk.

From this point the elevated circuit of Loch Skeen begins, first west along the boundary fence and wall to Firthybrig Head 2,504 feet, taking care not to stray too close to the rim of the rocky crag on the left. At the summit of Firthybrig Head swing south for 300 yards,

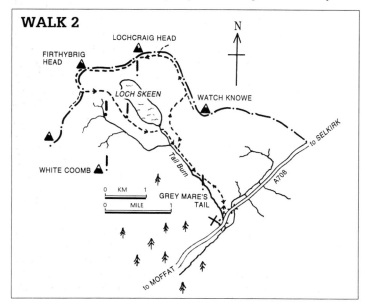

then leave the guiding fence to cross an open fell south-east, ie. left, to join the rock strewn ridge that encloses the western banks of Loch Skeen. Rather ragged along the top but with a good path, the ridge descends sharply at its southern tip, to join and ford the Tail Burn at the out-fall from Loch Skeen (easy in summer but troublesome in winter). A well constructed path leaves Loch Skeen behind and marches south-east to join the outward path above the Grey Mare's Tail. Descend slowly for the last mile to the car park at the side of the A708 road. The views of the glaciated Moffat Water Glen, with its spectacular waterfalls and the steep sided Bodesbeck Ridge opposite, are indeed breathtaking.

Accommodation and food are available in Moffat and around St Mary's Loch for Walks 2 and 2A.

WALK 2A. GREY MARE'S TAIL - LOCH SKEEN - MIDLAW BURN GORGE - DONALD'S CLEUCH HEAD - FIRTHYBRIG HEAD - LOCHCRAIG HEAD - TAIL BURN - GREY MARE'S TAIL

A variation of Walk 2, for those who relish the challenge of a rocky gorge scramble, followed by an elevated circuit of Loch Skeen.

This gorge walk with its accompanying waterslides, whilst embracing all the scenic grandeur of Walk 2, goes just "that little bit further". The total ascent is 2,154 feet, and in the gorge and on some sections of open fell there are no paths. Midlaw Burn Gorge (4) rises 250 feet from mouth to head, and involves rough walking, crossing Midlaw Burn at least six times. The ascent out of the gorge involves a scramble up a stone shute. The round trip covers 7 miles, but as rough and pathless terrain has to be crossed the 6 hour walk is given a degree of difficulty of 4. On a clear day navigation is not difficult, nevertheless it is advisable to carry map and compass, and essential to wear the right gear. This is a very photogenic walk, so take the camera and a plentiful supply of film.

The start, and initial ascent past the falls of the Grey Mare's Tail (1) to the southern tip of Loch Skeen (2) are as in Walk 2. At the southern end of Loch Skeen (2), ford the Tail Burn to ascend with the distinct path to the western ridge above Loch Skeen. Three quarters of a mile after crossing Tail Burn a large boulder is met at the 1,900-

foot contour line. At this boulder turn left on a bearing of 280 degrees magnetic into a wilderness peppered with hummocks of glacial debris. Progress is easier if the 1,900 foot altitude is maintained to the mouth of Midlaw Burn Gorge (4), ¹/₂ mile west of the boulder.

The Gorge, GR 163162, is entered by a sheep trace on the north side of the burn, heed well the words of Edward Whymper, "Look well to each step." As the gorge begins its relentless squeeze and the boulders grow larger the cascading burn squirms between the rocky sides, a grim reminder of the force of winter water. On reaching the climactic head of the gorge the way ahead appears impenetrable, two water slides, one shooting over a large slab of rock ahead, the other surging over slabs and scree to the left, bar the way. A steep scramble up a narrow stone shute on the left, parallel to the water slide cascading in from the left, will reward the experienced and determined mountaineer; an ascent via the waterfall ahead should be ignored. If conditions are not perfect for the ascent

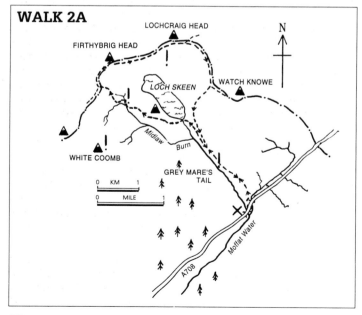

WALK 2A

LOCHCRAIG HEAD

FIRTHYBRIG HEAD

N

LOCH SKEEN

WATCH KNOWE

Midlaw Burn

WHITE COOMB

GREY MARE'S TAIL

0   KM   1

0   MILE   1

A708

Moffat Water

up the stone shoot, ie. excess water or ice, retrace your steps to the second curve in the burn and ascend the easier south side, ie. right, to the top rim. Should this climb not be acceptable return to the mouth, and ascend on the south rim to above the head of the gorge at GR 161163.

From this point on a bearing of 280° magnetic tramp over the open fell for $^1/_2$ mile to reach the fence/dyke at Donald's Cleuch Head 2,510 feet. On this flat and indistinguishable summit, GR 156164, turn immediately right and follow the helpful fence north for $^1/_2$ mile to Firthybrig Head 2,504 feet. Here the guiding fence turns sharp right, ie. east-north-east, to descend to a peat clad col before ascending steeply to the flat summit of Lochcraig Head (3) 2,625 feet. This peak must surely be one of the most noble grandstands in the Tweedsmuir Hills.

The descent turns right, ie. south from the summit with the stone dyke, and is so abrupt that care is needed for the next $^3/_4$ mile. In poor visibility always keep the dyke/fence in sight, for the south face of Lochcraig Head (3) is dangerously precipitous. The path by the fence once the level ground is reached is a mixture of peat and heather, with Loch Skeen now only 100/200 yards to the right. Halfway along the loch the fence swings left, ie. south-east, and it is here a thin path leaves the fence to continue south over heather covered mounds for $^1/_2$ mile, to join the path and the Tail Burn at the southern end of Loch Skeen. The luxury of a good path is the walker's reward as it descends with the picturesque and noisy Grey Mare's Tail (1) for 1 mile south-east.

Items of Interest Along the Way

(1) GREY MARE'S TAIL. A waterfall of outstanding size and power, and a tourist attraction of some note, named after the "Grey Mare" in Robert Burns's poem Tam o' Shanter. A statistic for the rock climber - two climbing routes up each side of the waterfall were pioneered by Edinburgh climbers during the severe winter of February 1969, in a climb of 450 feet.

(2) LOCH SKEEN. Set in a wild and desolate moor pimpled by glacial deposits and ringed by rocky mountain crags of some presence Loch Skeen, lying at 1,700 feet, is $^3/_4$ mile from north to south, its dark waters sinking to a depth of over 25 fathoms/

150 feet. Loch Skene (nineteenth-century spelling), was visited by Sir Walter Scott (which part of the Borders was not?) who, with his companion and their horses, was caught in the folds of a clinging mist: "as we were groping through a maze of bogs the ground gave way, and down went horse and horsemen pell-mell into a slough of peaty mud and black water, it was no easy matter to get extricated." Today the traveller has the talisman of the guidebook to help him on his way, and the walker can be assured that on a fine day the loch is a jewel in the crown of the Moffat Hills.

(3) LOCHCRAIG HEAD 2,625 feet. A fine flat topped mountain, capped in short grass and strewn with scattered sandstone, whose exposed rocky south face drops dramatically for 400 feet to the north shore of Loch Skeen. Third in height of the Moffat Hills, it provides a superb grandstand from which to view the surrounding peaks of the Southern Uplands.

(4) MIDLAW BURN GORGE, 2,250 feet. Its upper reaches contain several spectacular water slides, shooting and sliding down huge slabs of rock. The stony scramble of 250 feet, ascending with Midlaw Burn, is a pleasure not often offered to the mountaineer in these well rounded and fully clothed hills.

WALK 3. CARRIFRAN GR 159115 - CARRIFRAN BURN - CORRIE OF GUPE CRAIG - WHITE COOMB - CARRIFRAN GANS - CARRIFRAN

The hidden glen of Carrifran, second of the three lateral valleys that grace the Moffat Hills, digs deep into the central plateau, providing a fine valley walk culminating in the ascent of White Coomb 2,695 feet, the highest mountain in the range. A total ascent of 2,355 feet over 7 miles with a journey time of 5 hours, covers this grade 4 adventure. Conditions underfoot vary, from wide farm tracks to narrow sheep traces, though the upper reaches of these hills, unlike one or two of the Cheviots, provide dry and easy walking. Mountain clothing must be worn, and a map and compass carried, together with food and drink. A camera, preferably with a wide angle lens, is recommended.

Start the walk at Carrifran GR 159115, on the A708 road 7 miles north-east of Moffat. Parking on this narrow and twisting road presents a minor problem, there being only room for four cars, one on the grass verge at the south side of the bridge over Carrifran Burn, the others alongside the cattle grid opposite the white house of Carrifran.

Carrifran, at 571 feet above sea level, is the start of the walk. From the gate into the mouth of this impressive valley join the track leading north and running parallel to the Carrifran Burn. For the first mile the path rises 330 feet, for the second mile 550 feet, to the corrie between Raven Craig (1) and Gupe Craig. This gradual ascent is a fine introduction to the glen, running between rock and grassy ridge; Under Saddle Yoke 2,445 feet and Raven Craig (1) 2,247 feet

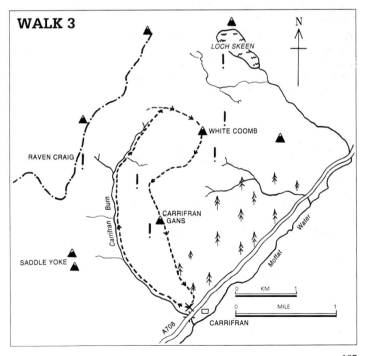

WALK 3

N

LOCH SKEEN

WHITE COOMB

RAVEN CRAIG

Carrifran Burn

CARRIFRAN GANS

SADDLE YOKE

Moffat Water

KM

MILE

A708

CARRIFRAN

Carrifran Glen

to the west, Carrifran Gans 2,452 feet and Gupe Craig 2,200 feet to the east.

Using the right, ie. east flank of Carrifran Burn, with its series of water slides as a guide, clamber north and at a fork in the burn swing right to follow the main burn north-north-east. At the 2,000 foot contour the steep slope levels off, with the rounded bulk of White Coomb (2) 2,696 feet rising ¹/₂ mile ahead. In good visibility leave the burn, turn half right, ie. north-east, and make an easy ascent across the open fell to the summit. Should conditions be poor with limited visibility continue to follow the burn to its source, and when a fence/dyke is met turn right, to follow it east-south-east to the summit.

Below White Coomb, 1 mile to the south-south-west, the flat and green top of Carrifran Gans (3) is easily reached on a path that drops to the dividing col then rises gently to the twin cairned summit. The descent south of 1¹/₂ miles from Carrifran Gans is straightforward, albeit steep in places, as it drops 1,880 feet to the road below, with the final leg following a boundary fence of patchy woodland apparently suffering from an attack of "arborial alopecia". Keep an eye open for the herd of feral goats (4) who dwell on these slopes. *Moffat and St Mary's Loch provide the nearest comforts.*

Items of Interest Along the Way

(1) RAVEN CRAIG. These dramatic cliffs rise for 500 feet at the head of the glen, and, coupled with Priest Craig, form a formidable barrier of rock stretching for 1 mile. Home to the peregrine falcon and the raven, these crags are the result of lateral glacial activity.

(2) WHITE COOMB 2,696 feet. White Coomb is spacious on top, providing an excellent vantage point from which to admire the entire panorama of the Southern Uplands and the Border Hills. Its western aspect slopes gently and easily to three outliers, not so to the north and east, where the descent is sudden and precipitous at Rough Craigs and Coomb Craig.

(3) CARRIFRAN GANS 2,543 feet. Provides spectacular views of the glen below and the twin cones of Saddle Yoke on the opposite ridge. The western flank of Carrifran Gans drops dramatically, and in poor visibility is dangerous to approach. Two small cairns a hundred or so yards apart adorn the summit, each appearing to be higher than the other.

(4) FERAL GOATS. Outcasts from the domestic scene these semi-wild goats roam the Border Hills and Southern Uplands. Running in small herds of around twenty, poor feeding and severe winters tend to keep the numbers low (though their diet is now supplemented by tourist's debris around the car parks of the Grey Mare's Tail). They can also be seen near Dob's Linn (Walk 1), and Black Craig (Walk 4).

WALK 4. CAPPLEGILL - SADDLE YOKE - RAVEN CRAIG - HARTFELL RIG - HART FELL - SWATTE FELL - BLACK CRAIG - CAPPLEGILL

An impressive and challenging high level walk, as an example of mountain scenery it may lack a little in height, but it certainly lacks nothing in form.

This 10 mile adventure has its hardest slog in the first 2 miles in the initial ascent of 1,945 feet, the remaining 8 miles involving only a minor ascent of 500 feet. Graded 4, the journey can take between 5 and 7 hours depending on conditions and time spent sight-seeing, taking photographs, bird-spotting or other high level activities. This is a high exposure walk, so be prepared.

Capplegill, a white and tidy farm 5¹/₂ miles north-east of the market town of Moffat, stands by the A708 road. Parking is never easy on this narrow and twisting road, but limited space is available on the wide grass verge at the east end of the shepherd's cottage (easily identified by the barking collies).

The initial 2 mile climb begins by the five-bar gate a few yards east of the white-washed cottage; follow the track north for 200 yards to a round sheep shelter on the right. Swing right leaving the main track to pass the stone stell and reach a gate in the fence to the east. Once through the gate the sharp sloping shoulder to Saddle

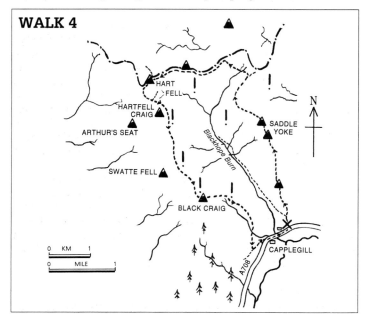

WALK 4

HART FELL

HARTFELL CRAIG

ARTHUR'S SEAT

SWATTE FELL

BLACK CRAIG

Blackhope Burn

SADDLE YOKE

CAPPLEGILL

A708

N

0   KM   1

0   MILE   1

Yoke rises to the north, nearly 2 miles ahead and 1,900 feet above, and the serious business of the climb to the summit of Saddle Yoke (1) 2,413 feet begins. Initially, paths are at best faint and thin, though if the north bearing is adhered to the trace becomes more distinct as height is gained. On reaching the grass covered peak, the Siamese twin of Under Saddle Yoke (1) 2,445 feet, can be seen. The path over the narrow and windy col is distinct and quite safe, though this section is not recommended for vertigo sufferers.

From the twin peaks walk north to a fork in the trace, take the right hand path to cross a flat and wet plateau north-east above the rim of the cliffs of Raven Craig (2). Proceed north-east to an unnamed summit 2,247 feet, bisected by the regional boundary fence/dyke. Turn left at the fence and using it as a guide follow it first north, and then west, through heather and hag passing the hardly noticed Hartfell Rig 2,432 feet, for $2^{1/2}$ long miles to the summit of Hart Fell (3) 2,651 feet. Hart Fell is marked by a rather small and untidy shelter cairn.

From the summit cairn a fence leads south, and then steeply east, before ascending to Hartfell Craig, where a delightful ridge walk of great presence begins its $3^{1/2}$ mile journey south to Capplegill. The traverse of Swatte Fell 2,390 feet, travels along the rim of its subsidiaries Falcon Craig 2,373 feet, Upper Coomb Craig 2,339 feet, Nether Coomb Craig 2,373 feet and Black Craig 2,150 feet. A path that is in places perilously close to the edge of the crags, but provides the walker (with a head for heights), with maximum views of Blackhope Valley and Whirly Gill. At Falcon Craig and Black Craig the path is perhaps too close to the edge, and in strong winds should be avoided by retreating well to the west.

On the descent from Black Craig the trail grows faint as a burn on the right is met. Cross the burn, and make for a gate in the electric fence ahead. Descend steeply south-south-west on a grassy path above the farm of Capplegill turning left onto a broad farm track. When the steading is reached turn left onto the A708 road to return to the shepherd's cottage. *Fish and chips and a selection of beds are available in Moffat and around St Mary's Loch.*

Items of Interest Along the Way

(1) SADDLE YOKE 2,413 feet, and UNDER SADDLE YOKE 2,445

feet. The twin peaks of Saddle Yoke are somewhat of a rarity amongst the rounded flat-topped hills of Tweedsmuir. Joined by a narrow and quite exciting little ridge, these steep sided mountains, with their distinctive and pointed peaks, still remain grass clad. Saddle Yoke is named only on the one-inch OS map, and Under Saddle Yoke the higher of the twins is named only on the OS 1:50,000 sheet. To capture the most effective and dramatic photographs of the sweeping ridges that circumnavigate this glen it is wise to harness the morning light.

(2) INHABITANTS OF THE MOFFAT HILLS. These hills are designated by the Nature Conservancy as being of special interest. Keep an eye open for ravens, buzzards, peregrine falcons and red grouse. By the lower burns herons, ring ouzels, dippers, wagtails and sandpipers can be seen. Mammals include mountain hares, fox, otter, feral goats and now feral mink are spreading.

(3) HART FELL 2,651 feet. The second highest of the Moffat Hills, giving pole position to White Coomb by a mere 44 feet, is a hill of many flat ridges that reward the walker with far reaching views. In clear and crisp air, over the silvery waters of the Solway Firth, the peaks of the northern English Lakes signal a greeting, and one winter's day through air of great clarity I had the good fortune to see the snow capped summit of Ben More 3,852 feet, 85 miles north.

WALK 5. TALLA WATER GR 143201 - GAMES HOPE GLEN - GREAT HILL - DONALD'S CLEUCH HEAD - FIRTHYBRIG HEAD - MOLLS CLEUCH DOD - TALLA WATER - GR 143201

This is a walk of two halves, each half equally appealing yet distinctly different. The first 3½ miles in the narrow confines of the wild and lonely glen of Games Hope, the second half, after a steep ascent of Great Hill 2,541 feet, is an explosion of Southern Upland scenery. Graded 3, the 8-mile journey, with a total ascent of 1,700 feet, will take 5 hours. Pathways vary from good to faint. A compass and map are needed in poor visibility, and weather proof clothing is essential for winter walking.

On the narrow road between the reservoirs of Megget and Talla a small lay-by at GR 143201 can take 5 or 6 cars. The walk starts at this point, crossing the stone bridge that straddles Talla Water then descending west on the narrow road for ¹/₂ mile to the mouth of Gameshope Glen. Talla Reservoir lies below curving gracefully north-west.

When Games Hope Burn (1) is reached a five-bar gate on the left marks the entrance to the glen. The farm track south is wide and easy underfoot, with the fascinating burn hurrying by on the right, and savage boulder fields covering the sides of Carlavin Hill. After 1¹/₂ miles a rickety wooden bridge over the burn to the collapsing cottage of Gameshope (take care with both structures) is reached.

Ahead a new fodder store marks an indistinct trace south by the east side of the burn. For the next mile the valley floor widens, and then for the first time since leaving Gameshope Farm, past the confluence of Donald's Cleuch Burn, the walking is better if the burn-side route is abandoned. Walk south-south-east, ie. diagonally across the plateau passing the occasional peat hag, and after 200 yards a track is met. Turn right, and follow the track south as far as a gate in the broken fence; a small wooden sheep pen and a metal fodder shed lie to the south.

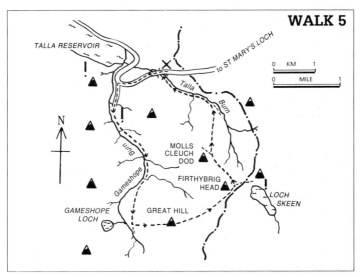

Above to the east is the rounded dome of Great Hill (2) 2,541 feet, with a post and wire fence for navigation the short sharp climb of 750 feet takes ¹/₂ to ³/₄ hour. The summit marks the start of 2 miles of fine ridge walking. Follow the dilapidated fence south-east to the col below, at its lowest point turn east, ie. left, and leave the fence to join a pathway above Donald's Cleuch (3). Three hundred and fifty yards ahead another fence with an accompanying stone wall (both in need of repair), is met; turn left and follow the fence to the peak of Firthybrig Head 2,504 feet. When the summit is reached a T-junction in the wall signals the point to leave the regional boundary fence and travel north-west alongside a broken wall for ³/₄ mile to the flat grassy summit of Molls Cleuch Dod 2,572 feet.

The northern rig of Molls Cleuch Dod descends gently for 1 mile to lead the walker to the floor of the Talla Water Valley, where a wide stony farm track heads westwards to the stone bridge and the end of the the walk.

Refreshments and accommodation can be found at St Mary's Loch and Tweedsmuir.

Items of Interest Along the Way

(1) GAMES HOPE BURN. For the first ¹/₂ mile or so it remains a rather ordinary mountain burn, however once beyond the point where the boulder strewn hillsides close in a transformation takes place. From a gurgling benign burn it changes into a brawling torrent, surging as if in panic from linn to linn, in a matter of seconds. On all sides the air is filled with a symphony of running water. Higher still as the valley opens out the burn changes again, murmuring softly here and there as if reluctant to disturb the solitude.

(2) THE PANORAMA FROM GREAT HILL. South - the hogsback of Hart Fell 2,651 feet, and the black crags of Swatte Fell 2,389 feet. Also the cones of Under Saddle Yoke 2,445 feet, and Saddle Yoke 2,413 feet probe dramatically skywards, with the flattened bulk of White Coomb 2,696 feet, to the left.

East - Donald's Cleuch Head 2,520 feet, Firthybrig Head 2,504 feet, and Lochcraig Head 2,625 feet.

North - Molls Cleuch Dod 2,572 feet, masks the giants of the Manor range.

West - Gameshope Loch, at 1,850 feet an elevated expanse of water with not one tree growing within sight. Above it the ridge of Garelet Dod 2,264 feet, and Garelet Hill 2,231 feet.

(3) DONALD'S CLEUCH. A wild and inhospitable place that spawns the burn of the same name. "Donald" refers to the Reverend Donald Cargill, minister of the Barony Church, Glasgow in 1665, who, deprived of his living for denouncing the Restoration, and fearing for his own safety, fled to these lonely and rugged hills. Here it is said, the Reverend Donald laid low for many months, well hidden from Claverhouse (the scourge of the Covenantors) and his prying dragoons. Heaven help them all, should they have been afoot on these mountains during winter's icy blast.

WALK 6. MEGGET STONE - FANS LAW - CAIRN LAW - BROAD LAW - PORRIDGE CAIRN - WYLIES HILL - MEGGET STONE

Unlike the wild corries and rocky crags of the Moffat Hills, the Manor's residents are composed of gentle slopes that favour an easy passage for the hill walker. Broad Law, at 2,754 feet the highest summit in the Borders, is an easy to ascend mountain that unfortunately has very little apart from the views to excite the explorer. The walk starts at 1,450 feet above sea level, which leaves an easy ascent of only 1,304 feet for the entire 6 miles. Graded 2, the walk will take no longer than 3½ hours to complete. Paths and navigation present no problems, though do pay the highest mountain in the range some respect by wearing your walking boots.

Parking for cars lies east of Talla Water bridge GR 143201, on the single track road connecting the reservoirs of Megget and Talla. Walk east for ½ mile to the cattle grid and the regional boundary close by the Megget Stone (1). To the north, ie. left, the continuous boundary fence staggers up the flank of Fan's Law, to ascend for 2 miles to the summit of Broad Law (2).

From Fan's Law, the boundary marker swings west and then north west to Cairn Law 2,353 feet. Cairn Law, its upper reaches scattered with well constructed cairns, directs the walker north alongside the fence for a gentle 1¼ mile ascent to the flat and wide western summit of Broad Law (2) 2,754 feet, capped with a metallic mushroom, whilst the lower eastern top 2,723 feet, $^1/_2$ mile north-east, sports a tall none too elegant radio mast, both erections the property of the Civil Aviation Authority.

At the mast leave the fence behind, and head right, ie. south-south-west, to the source of Wylies Burn 400 yards from the lower of Broad Law's twin summits. Once the source is reached walk south on the open fell keeping the same elevation, and also parallel to the boundary fence (used in the ascent of Broad Law). After $^1/_2$ mile the prominent Porridge Cairn 2,489 feet is reached. South-east of Porridge Cairn, a narrow and well defined ridge runs to Wylies Hill 1,996 feet, then descends sharply south to the narrow road close to a store shed, a total distance of $1^1/_2$ miles. The ridge is a fine and airy place to walk, and coupled with the

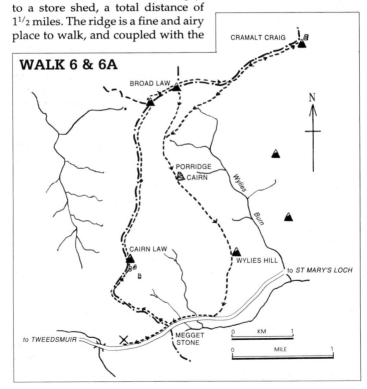

WALK 6 & 6A

descent on a well defined sheep trace, this stretch provides a wonderful feeling of solitude so characteristic of these hills.

At the road turn right, ie. west, and walk the last mile on the grass verges past the Megget Stone and the cattle grid, to the car park.

WALK 6A. AN ADDITIONAL 3 MILES OF WALKING, AND AN ADDITIONAL ASCENT OF 650 FEET TO THE SUMMIT OF CRAMALT CRAIG 2,723 FEET, THE SECOND HIGHEST SUMMIT IN THE MANOR HILLS

The journey to the mast on the lower summit of Broad Law is a carbon copy of Walk 6, and from this point the distinct top of Cramalt Craig (3) with its large cairn can be seen to the north east. When descending east from Broad Law keep close to the fence, and do not stray left, as the precipitous cliffs of Polmood Craig lurk unseen to the north. The fence that has been constant guide crosses a damp and peaty area before rising sharply to Cramalt Craig (3) 2,723 feet, 1½ miles away.

On the summit, the large cairn provides that little extra height from which to view the entire range of the Manor Hills, for it is at this point that we must turn and commence the return journey. Descend on the path of ascent as far as the col below Broad Law, and from the lowest point of the col contour south-west, across the open moor. Half a mile and 200 feet of ascent across the southern flank of Broad Law on faint sheep traces, to reach the source of Wylies Burn. Turn south, ie. left to Porridge Cairn, from where the remainder of the journey is exactly as in Walk 6. This variation extends the walk into a pleasant 5 hours. *Food and accommodation are available at St Mary's Loch.*

Items of Interest Along the Way (Walks 6 & 6A)

(1) MEGGET STONE. Standing over 3 feet high, the Megget Stone rests just south of the cattle grid. Although it bears some indistinct markings it appears to have no greater claim to fame than to be a simple boundary mark.

(2) BROAD LAW 2,754 feet. It is said the summit can be traversed by a sleeping babe in a push chair, so flat is the summit and so smooth the path. This may be so, nevertheless it is still worth the effort to walk the wide fells of this slumbering giant, especially after a light dusting of snow. On a more romantic note the spring known as Gedde's Well, gushing from the western heights of Broad Law, is reputed to be the spot where the "wizard Merlin was wont to rest".

(3) CRAMALT CRAIG 2,723 feet. The second of the great Manor hills, connected to the third, Dollar Law 2,681 feet, by a fine flat ridge that forms the western ridge of that most picturesque of valleys, Manor Water. A ridge that can be walked from Megget to Peebles, some 19 miles or so, by following the regional boundary and then a parish boundary. With such fiscal and spiritual guidance, who would not be encouraged to venture forth to Peebles.

WALK 7. TALLA BRIDGE GR 143201 - MUCKLE SIDE - MATHIESIDE CAIRN - VICTORIA LODGE (TALLA DAM) - TALLA LINNFOOTS - TALLA BRIDGE

An invigorating ridge and waterside walk; initially a rather demanding climb on open fellside, but once the 1,800 foot contour is reached the walking becomes easier. For the next 3 miles the views reveal what scenic riches lie hidden in the Borders. After a tranquil stroll by the reservoir's edge an ascent to Talla Linn, in all 8 short miles, 1,415 feet of ascent, graded barely 3, it will be accomplished in 5 hours. Take provisions, especially water, as no refreshments are available en route.

A narrow road with passing places connects the A708 at St Mary's Loch with the A701 at Tweedsmuir. West beyond Megget reservoir, a small parking space between the regional boundary and Talla Water bridge marks the starting point of the walk. Walk 50 yards west, to a small slip rail in the dry stone dyke on the right. Ascend the open hillside north (look out for weasels), to a cairn on the skyline, from where a second cairn is reached 100 yards ahead. Far below Talla Reservoir (1) can be seen snaking west. To the north-east some 300 yards ahead marker posts and a fence are now visible;

30 yards before reaching the fence turn left and walk parallel to it until it turns sharp right below Cairn Law.

At this right angle leave the fence and ascend north-west across the fellside, to join another fence above the distinct Y-shaped rocky gullies of Talla Cleuch. Once this second fence is reached navigation ceases to be a problem. Below, a farm in miniature, as Talla Linnfoots crouches behind a break of bent and battered trees. Follow the fence north-west, ascending steadily above the steep slopes of Muckle Side, to the summit of Talla Cleuch Head 2,265 feet. The fence side path leads north then west to a small outcrop, Mathieside Cairn 2,180 feet, an ideal spot to take a break. Descend west from Mathieside Cairn alongside the fence for 1 mile; a narrow path runs on the left of the fence close to the edge of the rig, giving more spectacular views of Talla Reservoir, (not recommended for vertigo sufferers). From this point the fence leads north-west alongside the trees to a line of telegraph poles, situated in the centre of a wide forest ride. Pass through a small wooden gate and descend north-north-west with the poles for 900 yards, to the ruin of a stone sheep shelter (enclosing a wood and plastic "hide").

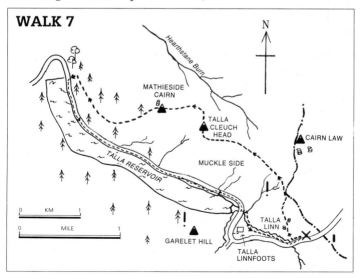

From the shelter walk 30 yards south-west to the deciduous trees surrounded by a black metal fence, 30 yards south-west the fence meets a coniferous plantation. At this point pass through the small gate to follow the fence as it descends west for approximately 100 yards, to the narrow road alongside the reservoir.

Once the road is reached turn left, ie. south and then south-east, for 3 miles to the farm of Talla Linnfoots. The roadside verge is wide and grassy, and even on a sunny Saturday in late August no more than a dozen motorised vehicles will trundle past. At Talla Linnfoots ascend with the crumbling path that scales the side of Talla Burn to Talla Linn (2). A steep but rewarding climb past the rowan trees and the purple heather, to the bridge and the end of the walk. *The nearest food and accommodation is at St Mary's Loch or Tweedsmuir.*

Items of Interest Along the Way

(1) TALLA RESERVOIR. Before the first World War Talla Water flowed through a deep and swampy valley. Today, one mile south of Tweedsmuir church, a great concrete barrier straddles the valley, and beyond that stretches three miles of reservoir to Talla Linnfoot. Time has smoothed the sorrow of a drowned valley, and now the good folk of Edinburgh have their water, and the Borders has another loch.

Who knows if "Young Hay of Talla's" pele tower lies buried deep in a watery grave.

> "Winter night raving,
> Young Hay of Talla,
> Snowy drift smooring,
> Loud the Linn roaring,
> Young Hay of Talla."

Hay was one of two executed on 3rd January 1568 for the murder of Darnley.

(2) TALLA LINN. By these multiple waterfalls close to the leaning rowans the Covenanters held a secret meeting in 1682, recorded by Sir Walter Scott, in "The Heart of Midlothian". Hard and dour, our Covenanting ancestors were not blessed with tolerance, as is aptly stated in the old verse,

> "prove their doctrine orthodox
> By apostolic blows and knocks."

WALK 8. LANGHAUGH - KIRKHOPE - LONG GRAIN KNOWE - PYKESTONE HILL - POSSO CRAIG - LANGHAUGH

Manor Water Valley is a picturesque valley typical of these parts, benign and welcoming on the valley floor, whilst at the same time gaunt and forbidding on the surrounding tops and ridges. It cannot be ignored. The walk circumnavigates 6½ miles of valley, hill and ridge, climbing 1,654 feet in 4 hours, and carries a degree of difficulty grading of 3. Underfoot the tracks, paths and traces are clear and mainly dry, though for the final section of Posso Craig steep slopes have to be negotiated. It is a walk that provides superb views, in an area steeped in history. Boots and mountain clothing are recommended, and in poor visibility a map and compass.

Leave the A72 road, 1½ miles west of Peebles, to enter the Manor Water Valley (signposted Manor and Manorhead). Travel south along the narrow unclassified road for 7 miles to GR 199308, a few hundred yards past the white buildings of Langhaugh on the

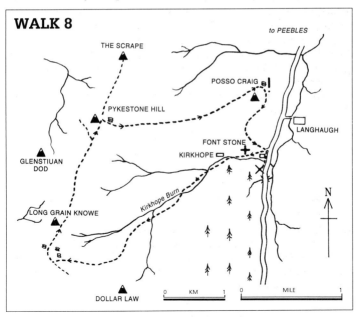

left. A solitary white cottage at GR 199308 marks the start of the walk, with parking available for six vehicles in a small lay-by between the cottage and a road bridge.

Take the farm track leading south-west to Kirkhope, and immediately the appetite is whetted. Posso Craig rising steeply to the right, with the domes of Pykestone Hill 2,415 feet, and Long Grain Knowe 2,308 feet, covering the skyline ahead; and if that's not enough the mysterious Font Stone (1) on its ancient plot comes into view on the right.

Three-quarters of a mile from the start the deserted cottage of Kirkhope is reached, skirt round the buildings to continue south-west on a grassy track running parallel to Kirkhope Burn. Follow the burn for approximately 1 mile until more sheep pens are reached; ford the burn onto a distinct path leading to the ridge by Newholm Hill, aiming left of the two visible cairns. Once the ridge is breasted bear right, ie. west, to the well defined and cairned jeep track known as Thief's Road (2). Turn right and ascend ¹/₂ mile north close to the parish boundary fence to reach the domed and rather dull summit of Long Grain Knowe.

The way continues alongside the fence at a brisk pace, rising and falling for 1 mile to a trig point marking the top of Pykestone Hill (3) 2,415 feet. Pykestone Hill is distinguished by a scattering of spear or pike-headed stones, protruding skywards, and includes a cairn which will act as a marker to the ridge of Posso Craig.

From the trig point on Pykestone Hill face the cairn, to follow a sometimes faint double track east for ³/₄ mile, descending steadily on the narrowing ridge to Posso Craig. To the north, the black and severe gully of Posso, to the south the more gentle glen of Kirkhope. Continue to lose height as the ridge swings north-east, ie. left, and the summit of Posso Craig (4) 1,859 feet, with its three piles of stones, is approached. It's a delightful spot from which to view the Manor Valley 1,000 feet below, but do take great care, DO NOT VENTURE PAST a large well made cairn standing on the northern rim of the summit. Beyond, the rock drops dramatically to the valley floor. Posso Craig gives the walk its difficulty grade 3.

From above the cairn, circle and descend south-east and then south-west around Posso Craig, dropping rapidly, using clear though narrow sheep traces to reach the valley floor at the white cottage GR 199308. *A wide selection of refreshments and beds are available in Peebles.*

Items of Interest Along the Way

(1) FONT STONE. Standing in a field, right of the track to Kirkhope, is the site of the ancient Kirk of St Gordian, now scarcely visible save for the grass covered foundations and the levelled ground. At its side stand the Font Stone (two foot across and hollowed out), and its guardian granite cross embellished with interwoven decorations (and marked Sanct Gordiani). Headstones are also present, their inscriptions masked with grey lichen.

(2) THIEF'S ROAD. As it reads, a way used in the past to drive "borrowed" cattle along, well above the preying eyes of the valley floor. Later to be used as a legitimate Drove Road.

(3) PYKESTONE HILL 2,415 feet. The summit of a four pointed star whose outlyers, Long Grain Knowe, Den Knowes Head, Breach Law and Posso Craig, radiate to the four points of the compass; and whose twin top, The Scrape, stands guard to the north. No doubt its name was derived from the sharp and pointed stones found in profusion on the summit.

(4) POSSO CRAIG 1,859 feet. The watchdog of Manor, below whose rocky eastern cliffs stands the Ship Stone, cliffs referred to in Scott's "Bride of Lammermuir" as the source of hunting hawks. It is a place to sit and ponder, and to admire the Manor Valley.

WALK 9. KIRKHOUSE - ORCHARD MAINS - GLEN HOUSE - GLENSHIEL BANKS - PEAT HILL - BLAKE MUIR - KIRKHOUSE

A walk combining the sylvan beauty of the glen of Quair Water with the invigorating open and empty spaces of the ridges of the eastern Manor Hills. The 10 mile walk has a difficulty grade of 2, and takes 5½ hours to complete, with 1,450 feet total ascent. Car parking presents a problem, the only possible place to leave a vehicle is by the farm buildings at Orchard Mains (1). Please check at the farm, to ensure no obstruction is caused.

Start the walk at Orchard Mains, having left the B709 road 1 mile south of Traquair at the right turn (signposted Glen House 1³/₄ miles, Orchard Mains). Follow the quiet country lane south-west and then west for 1 mile to the arched main gates of Glen House (2). At this point the tree lined right fork winds south-west to the rear of Glen House. When the metalled road ends a notice saying "Private" refers only to motorised vehicles; the route from Glen House to Glenshiel Banks is a pedestrian right of way. The turreted Glen House is passed on the left and at two cottages on the right take the right fork and follow the farm track south-west for two very pleasant miles, past woods and pastures, to the two cottages (one in use, the other a ruin) at Glenshiel Banks.

Pass through a five-bar gate ahead to the heather clad flanks of Peat Hill 1,550 feet. To the west, ie. right, the rounded cairn topped summit of Dun Rig 2,433 feet, can be seen, the highest top of this section of the Manor Hills. Once through the gate three pathways are visible, take the centre one and ascend Peat Hill south-south-

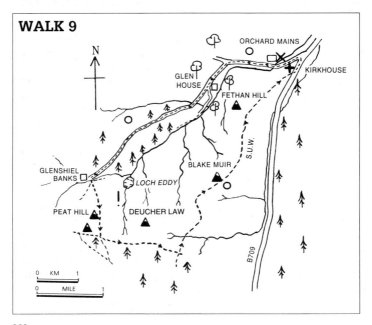

WALK 9

N

ORCHARD MAINS

GLEN HOUSE

KIRKHOUSE

FETHAN HILL

S.U.W.

GLENSHIEL BANKS

BLAKE MUIR

LOCH EDDY

PEAT HILL

DEUCHER LAW

B709

0   KM   1

0   MILE   1

Glenshiel Cottage

east. This steady climb affords fine views below and to the north of the picturesque glen of Quair Water, and the shimmering waters of Loch Eddy. On the highest point of the shoulder on Peat Hill, a single post indicates the path which continues to descend to the edge of a coniferous plantation. From Glenshiel Banks to the woodside boundary fence is 1 mile.

Turn left when the trees are met, climbing steadily east with the broken stone dyke to the shoulder of Deucher Law 1,680 feet. Descend east-south-east for $^1/_2$ mile (with a sheep stell to the left), to meet the Southern Upland Way cutting across the county boundary. Join this long distance path and travel north-north-east, ie. left, for nearly 4 miles over Blake Muir to Kirkhouse.

Cross Yellow Mire Burn, keeping it on the right, before taking the path on the left to the marker post (thistle) ahead. From this post the path to Blake Muir 1,512 feet is due north, and shortly before the summit the way broadens out into a distinct track. The moorland crossing to Blake Muir reveals some fine views of the folding ridges of Minch Moor, Brown Knowe and the outstanding cairns topping Three Brethren (Chapter 2, Walk 6, and Chapter 3, Walk 1).

Follow the ridge north, descending steadily between

embankments, alongside a fence, to the western corner of a lone plantation. Two more stiles are crossed as the way runs alongside a stone dyke, swinging north-east to descend to the B709 road near Kirkhouse. Walk north past the white Traquair Parish Church (3) for several hundred yards, turn left, ie. west, and cross the bridge over Quair Water to return to Orchard Mains. *Traquair and Innerleithen provide fuel and rest.*

Items of Interest Along the Way

(1) ORCHARD MAINS. The farm buildings, in particular the barn by the roadside, are well worth an inspection. At the road end leading to the farm a red Victorian letter-box, embossed with "Letters Only, VR" can be seen.

(2) GLEN HOUSE. The original house was the birthplace of one Captain John Porteous, whose infamous act of ordering the city guard of Edinburgh to open fire on the crowd at a public hanging in 1736, killing four, led to him being tried and sentenced to death. Granted a pardon by Queen Caroline, this act so incensed the populace they broke John Porteous out of the Tolbooth, hanged him from a street sign, breaking his neck. Another Porteous from these parts (no doubt an antecedent), gained infamy by slaughtering sixteen captive troopers from Cromwell's army in cold blood. An historian recorded it thus, "did cut off numberis of the Englishes, and seased thair pockettis and horssis."

(3) TRAQUAIR PARISH CHURCH. A kirk has stood on this spot since the early 1500s, the present building being built in 1778 and altered in 1821. The outside staircase is of interest (its like can be seen at Ettrick Kirk, Chapter 3, Walk 6), as are the many gravestones emblazoned with the skull and crossbones, and the graves headed with a single unmarked river boulder. The roadside wall of the church bears a memorial plaque to blacksmith Alexander Brodie of Traquair who died in 1811, and who invented "the register stoves and fire hearths for ships" as used by the Royal Navy.

WALK 10. PEEL - GLENKINNON BURN - BROOMY LAW - THREE BRETHREN - YAIR BRIDGE - PEEL

A delightful walk of ever opening vistas, combined with gentle progress alongside the Tweed. Said the Fairy Queen to Thomas the Rhymer,

> *"Gin ye wad meet wi' me again,*
> *Gang to the bonny banks o' Fairnilee,"*

A ramble of 7½ miles, with an easy and steady ascent of 1,123 feet, graded 2, and taking 5 hours. In dry summer conditions, thick soled trainers will be adequate. A camera is recommended.

Peel (1), is reached via the A707 Innerleithen to Selkirk road, crossing the Tweed to Peel and Ashiestiel over a narrow bridge. Limited parking is available immediately over the bridge, where a farm track (with cattle-grid) enters from the left.

Walk west, along the quiet tree lined road for ½ mile to the

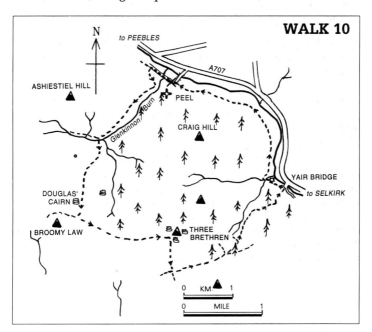

signposts "Williamhope" and "Beware of the Bull". Turn left at the junction and follow the road south, for 1¹/₂ miles. The statuesque Peel House is on the left, with the hurrying Glenkinnon Burn lined by a fine collection of deciduous trees. At the southern corner of the coniferous plantation on Craig Hill leave the road to turn left and pass through a five-bar gate 30 yards from the road.

A clear grassy track through the remnants of the deciduous trees fords Glenkinnon Burn, to wind south-east and then south (with the conifers always on the left), to Glenkinnon Ridge. At the first rise a metal five-bar gate opens to the open fell, where a grassy track winds south ascending through rushes, bracken and heather. As height is gained a large stone, William's Cross (2), can be seen to the right, and ahead two sad and lonely trees signal a large cairn (2) on the skyline. This cairn is not only of great interest, but also acts as a marker. Continue south past the square cairn to breast the ridge and meet the Southern Upland Way.

Turn left, ie. east, and follow the clear path between dyke and plantation to the distinctive three cairns on Three Brethren (3) 1,523 feet. Descend south-east, with the forest still on the left and a fence on the right. The Way is clearly waymarked as it crosses two tracks to descend north-east to a clump of beech trees on the left. Swing left onto a wide track and join the forest walk through Lindinny Wood. In addition to the thistle waymarks the Forestry Commission has placed several information boards by the path descending to the A707 road and Yair Bridge (4).

Do not cross the bridge, but continue on the south side of the river Tweed on the road marked "Private Road" to Yair House (4). After ¹/₂ mile the road forks, go left avoiding the main entrance to Yair House, around the west end of the private grounds, and then turn right to travel north with the Tweed. The 2 mile walk over a wide farm track travels with the river, turning west once the corner of Craig Hill is rounded. It is a walk of charm and tranquillity, returning via the last cattle grid to Peel. *Accommodation etc. is obtainable nearby at Clovenfords.*

Items of Interest Along the Way

(1) PEEL. The site of a hospital built during the 1939-1946 conflict, later to act as a general hospital serving the Borders region until the

1980s. The mansion of Peel House can be seen through the trees, and a little distance west stands Ashiestiel on the banks of the Tweed, home of Sir Walter Scott before Abbotsford, "Here were spent the seven happiest years of his life."

(2) WILLIAM'S CROSS and CAIRN. The "cross" is in reality a great stone positioned south of Glenkinnon Burn, reputed to be the spot where Sir William Hope Douglas "Knight of Liddesdale" was put to the sword by a kinsman in 1353. Half a mile to the south and 350 feet above the "cross" stands a square cairn, 7 feet high and topped with a single stone on its edge. A plaque disputes the position of William's Cross "By Tradition, This is where Sir W Hope Douglas was slain" Glendinning 1913. Sir W.Hope Douglas was also known as "Flower of Chivalry", a title he ill deserved for in 1342 he dragged Sir Alexander Ramsay, the Sheriff of Teviotdale, from the sheriff's court in Hawick, incarcerating him in Hermitage Castle. Sir Alexander starved to death in seventeen days.

(3) THREE BRETHREN. A fine vantage point capped by three very fine conical cairns, built to mark the limits of the estates of Yair, Philiphaugh and the burgh of Selkirk. From this distinctive top the rolling hills of the Borders flow gently to distant horizons.

(4) YAIR BRIDGE, YAIR HOUSE. Built in 1762 to replace a ford near the mouth of Caddon Water, it has been repaired many times but never widened. A narrow structure with no footpath, its three arches remain exactly as they were in 1762.

Yair House stands on the south bank of the Tweed surrounded by elegant deciduous trees. Built in 1788, it took its name from the hill and the forest of Yair to the west. On the opposite river bank is the haunting ruin of Fernilee where Alison Rutherford wrote her matchless version of *The Flowers of the Forest*. The room where she wrote is preserved to this day.

Chapter 5:
Long Distance Walks and Town Trails

Three long distance paths pass through the Borders, the Pennine Way, the Alternative Pennine Way and the Southern Upland Way. The much publicised Pennine Way is covered by a wide selection of guides including one for the Alternative Way. The less publicised Southern Upland Way has fewer though all are readily available from bookshops, outdoor shops and public libraries. Booklets with local information describing the town trails are also available from tourist information centres, at prices ranging from 10p to 50p. It is therefore intended to give only the briefest of descriptions in this chapter, in the hope that the appetite for walking the long distance paths and the town trails will be stimulated further.

THE PENNINE WAY

A high level walk, the dream of Tom Stephenson, past secretary of the Ramblers Association, became a reality in 1965. Stretching 270 miles north from Edale in Derbyshire, it traverses the backbone of England to complete its last 29 miles on the windswept ridges of the Cheviot Hills to Kirk Yetholm, The Borders, Scotland. Ten walks in Chapter 1 tread this long distance path, although only six travel its well worn way for any appreciable distance.

> *Maps:*   *OS 1:50,000 Landranger series, Sheets 74 and 80.*
> *Publication:*   *The Pennine Way Companion, by A.Wainwright, published by Michael Joseph.*

From Byrness in Redesdale to Kirk Yetholm in Roxburghshire there are 27 high level miles, 29 long miles if the summit of The Cheviot is included. The Way zig-zags and undulates with the national boundary fence for most of the journey, and never passes shelter save for two small wooden refuges on the slopes of Lamb Hill and Auchope Cairn. It is a testing walk, only to be undertaken in a single trip by fit and experienced walkers. Given good weather and clear skies, the rewards are high. Endless folds of grass and heather clad hills surrounded by the patchwork of the Northumbrian coastal plain and the Tweed Valley reward the walker tenfold. In recent years much of the sting has been taken out of the more sadistic sections, by wooden walk-ways and stone paths constructed across the peaty wastes, causing great relief to some and extreme annoyance to the purists.

The spectacular gorge of the Hen Hole Chapter 1 Walk 7, and the ascent of Cheviot, 2,676 feet in Chapter 1 Walks 9 and 9A, are covered in detail as are the tops of Windy Gyle 2,034 feet, Mozie Law, and Beefstand Hill in Chapter 1 Walks 10 and 14. The section Black Halls and Brownhart Law to the Roman Encampment at Chew Green is described in Chapter 1 Walk 15.

THE ALTERNATIVE PENNINE WAY

This walk of 431km from Ashbourne in Derbyshire to Jedburgh in Scotland is the invention of Denis Brook and Phil Hinchliffe. It takes an easier walking line than the original, with accommodation available at every stage.

Maps: OS 1:50,000 Landranger series, Sheets 74 and 800
Publication: The Alternative Pennine Way, by D.Brook and P. Hinchliffe published by Cicerone Press.

The route approaches the Borders from Nenthead, via Allendale Town, Haltwhistle, and over Hadrian's Wall to Falstone and Kielder, then through the forest to Byrness and so to Jedburgh. There is an extension to Melrose for those who wish to prolong the walk!

THE SOUTHERN UPLAND WAY

Extends for 202 miles on Scottish soil, running from Portpatrick on the west coast to Cockburnspath on the east coast. Opened in 1984, it is Scotland's first long distance path to run from coast to coast. Although not as rugged as the Western Highlands, the Southern Upland Way climbs to heights that exceed any point on the West Highland Way (Scotland's most popular long distance path).

Eighty-five and a half miles of this rather new well waymarked path enters the Borderland at Ettrick Head, by the "Welcome to Borders

Region" sign, and finishes at Cockburnspath on the Berwickshire coast.

Several of its most picturesque and interesting sections are incorporated into a selection of the walks, in Chapters 2, 3 and 4. In all a total of 8 walks in the guide cover sections from Ettrick Head to Yair Bridge.
Maps: OS 1:50,000 Landranger series, Sheets 79, 73, 74 and 67.
Publication: A Guide to the Southern Upland Way, by David Williams published by Constable and Co. Ltd.

The eastern section of this coast to coast long distance walk enters the area at Ettrick Head, a wild and lonely col 1,700 feet above sea level. The Way covers lonely hills, romantic glens and that oft praised loch of St Mary's, in addition to the banks of the silvery Tweed. A quiet route with no problematic navigation that draws the intrepid traveller ever onwards. In the words of James Hogg, "That's the Way for Billy and me."

From the exposed col of Ettrick Head the Way descends north-east into the shelter of Ettrick Water Valley, Chapter 3, Walk 9A, which soon joins a section of Chapter 3 Walk 6 at the farm of Scabcleuch. The twin jewels of Loch of the Lowes and St Mary's Loch are included in Chapter 3 Walk 4, and the open fells to Dryhope and Blackhouse, where dark and dreadful deeds took place in centuries past, are fully described in Chapter 3 Walk 3. A climb north-east to the fine ridge of Blake Muir, Chapter 4 Walk 9, leads to the village of Traquair, the start of Chapter 2 Walk 6, before ascending the drove road of Minch Moor. From Minch Moor past the mysterious Wallace's Trench at Browne Knowe 1,718 feet, Chapter 3 Walk 1, is another fine ridge walk to the summit of Three Brethren, from where Chapter 4 Walk 10 takes the wayfarer down to the Tweed at Yair Bridge.

BERWICK UPON TWEED, TOWN AND RIVER TRAILS

Exploring Berwick - *Berwick Visitors Guide No. 4, and* The Tweed Estuary Circular Walk, *published by the Berwick Ramblers, are available from local tourist information centres for 20p and 25p respectively.*
Exploring Berwick *contains two trails, the first a complete circuit of the unique town walls whilst the second trail embraces the fascinating streets of the old town.*

The Tweed Estuary trail is a 5½ mile circular walk, providing fine views of this historic town and its three bridges, built 1634-1928.

Berwick changed hands no less than fourteen times in its turbulent past, and was under English control in the second half of the 1500s when the construction of the town walls began. At that time they represented the most advanced design known to military engineers, but due to the Union of the Crowns in 1603 the walls never experienced shot or shell fired in anger.

THE WALL TRAIL begins at Meg's Mount on the north wall, including Cumberland Bastion and Brass Bastion; turn south past Cow Port, Windmill Bastion to King's Mount. The bastions all have two "flankers", whilst the mounts have only one, (a "flanker" is a protected gun emplacement allowing fire along the face of the wall). From the east wall the views are to the sea and the river mouth, a fact reflected in the names of points of interest along the route, Pier Gate, Fishers Fort, Shore Gate and Quay Walls. From Quay Walls the walls pass by the Old Bridge and the Royal Tweed Bridge to return to Meg's Mount.

THE STREET TRAIL also starts at Meg's Mount and travels south into the main shopping street with the Town Hall, built in 1761, resplendent at its foot. From the Town Hall walk into Church Street, leading north to the Parade, the Parish Church (without a spire) and the Barracks (containing the Regimental Museum of the King's Own Scottish Borderers, the Borough Museum and Art Gallery with Berwick's Burrell Collection). South of the barracks Ravensdowne leads to Palace Green, Bridge Street and Quay Walls. An interesting end to the walk is to cross the old bridge to Tweedmouth, returning via the Royal Tweed Bridge.

TWEED ESTUARY CIRCULAR WALK. A circular walk of 3 hours, embracing both banks of the Tweed estuary, with fine views of Berwick and its surrounds. In particular the Royal Border Bridge (a railway bridge), with its elegant arches, designed and built by Robert Stephenson and opened in 1850 by Queen Victoria.

KELSO TOWN TRAIL

Kelso Town Trail, *available from the tourist information centre for 50p. This comprehensive fourteen page booklet contains three walks through the ancient market town, each walk telling a historical, ecclesiastical and trading story. The town, of some 6,500 inhabitants, stands by two rivers, the Tweed and the Teviot, and proudly boasts two castles and an abbey. Kelso is renowned for its livestock sales, the Border Union Agricultural Show, and in recent years national and international honours for its fine floral displays. The walks start and finish in the picturesque square at the town's centre.*

THE ABBEY WALK. Includes the abbey, an interesting bridge by James Rennie, a riverside walk and the octagonal old parish church.

THE MARKET WALK. Starting south of the Town Hall by a group of Georgian houses, it travels along Woodmarket to the Coalmarket (an area of the town where coal mined south of Berwick upon Tweed was sold), turning into Horsemarket to return to the square.

THE UPPER TOWN. Leaves the square on the north side passing the fine facade of the Library, and the old Ragged School (initially a school for children of the poor), past two churches and the old Kelso Dispensary, established in 1777. Returning to the town centre via the banks of the Tweed and Cunzie, which was either the town mint or the place from where coins were distributed.

JEDBURGH TOWN TRAIL

The booklet Jedburgh Town Trail is available from the tourist information centre for 30p.

The Royal Burgh of Jedburgh (granted by King William the Lion 1143-1214), now home to 4,200, had its origins 3,000 years ago. It grew in stature and importance with the founding of its Augustinian Abbey in 1138. An abbey that was sacked and rebuilt many times before its final demise under the sword of the Earl of Hertford in 1545. Centuries of repeated destruction failed to quell the spirit of "Jethart", and destruction has slowly given way to construction, although some of the more macabre happenings from the past are still remembered, such as the game of "Hand-ba". This was a form of coarse rugby played by the "Uppies and the Doonies" of the town. The original "ba's", were said to be the severed heads of English soldiers, which were then thrown and kicked around the streets. The annual contest takes place every February.

Contained in the trail booklet is a map of this compact town, showing in detail the points of interest along the way. The trail starts at the Market Place, passes Newgate (once a prison with a condemned cell), to the visitors' centre of Jedburgh Abbey. After completing a tour of the abbey walk up Castlegate, passing Bonnie Prince Charlie's House and Abbey Close, to reach Castle Jail. Return to the Market Place and travel north through High Street to Mary Queen of Scots' House, a fine example of a sixteenth-century Border fortified house. Continue to the riverside for examples of buildings that supplied the towns water, the towns defences and housed the Burgh's pipers.

A WALK AROUND MELROSE

A Walk Around Melrose containing details of two walks around the town, complete with comprehensive maps, is available for 50p from the local tourist information centre.

Melrose, dominated by the distinctive triple peaks of the Eildon Hills (Chapter 2, Walk 5), was first settled by the ancient tribe of Selgovae some 2,000 years ago, later to be followed by the Romans at Trimontium (camp of the three hills). Centuries later the Celtic Christians established a monastery at Mailros (a bare headland) where Cuthbert, a local shepherd, was to start his monastic life. In 1136 King David founded the Cistercian Abbey, the ruins of which bear sad witness to the deeds of the Earl of Hertford who, in 1545, reduced this most humorous of Abbeys to the building you see today. The humour is supplied by the many fine carvings and gargoyles seen on the skyline, such as a pig playing the bagpipes. Priorwood Gardens close by the Abbey specialises in an Apple Orchard through the Ages, and flowers suitable for drying. During the eighteenth century the town was famous for the fine linen it produced, and in 1883 the game of Rugby Sevens was introduced to the world by Ned Haigh, a local butcher.

The INNER CIRCLE walk starts at the abbey car park and encompasses Abbey Street, the Market Square, High Street and Buccleuch Street. It includes such items as the Market Cross, 1645, the Town Hall, the Corn Exchange, the George and Abbotsford Hotel and Leslie House, before returning to the abbey and its most interesting museum.

The OUTER CIRCLE walk also starts at the abbey car park to follow the route of the Inner Circle walk as far as the High Street. Pass St Mary's Preparatory School and the famous Greenyards, home of Melrose Rugby Football Club (once a post glacial lake, later rough grazing and an area for selling sheep), to reach higher ground and the Parish Church. To the east is the Chain Bridge circa 1826, allowing foot traffic to cross to and from Gattonside, passing the Melrose Motor Museum before returning to the starting point.

GALASHIELS OLD TOWN WALK and WALKS IN GALA COUNTRYSIDE

Two small guides with maps, Galashiels Old Town Walk *by Ian M. Miller, and* Walks in Gala Countryside *by B and M.E.Lennox, both priced at 30p are available from the tourist information centre.*

Galashiels, a town of some 14,000 souls, is steeped in the woollen trade. The Galashiels Manufacturers Corporation, founded in 1776, spun the motto "We Dye to Live and Live to Die". So highly thought of is the Scottish College of Textiles based in the town, that in 1991 it became a college of Heriot Watt University, Edinburgh.

Galashiels Old Town Walk, is a compact stroll around the tight knit perimeter of the old town of Gala, a settlement dating from the fifteenth century. It embraces Old Gala House, on the site of the original manor house, Gala Town Cross, Gala Parish Church and Scott Aisle. Galashiels, invariably referred to throughout the Borders as Gala, appears to have escaped the extremes of violence experienced by other Border towns in centuries past, though the area known as "Whitchyknowe" witnessed the firing of "Whitches" in both the sixteenth and seventeenth centuries.

Start at Old Gala House, now a museum and exhibition centre, then walk to Scott Park (the site of New Gala House, built 1876, demolished 1985). The route then proceeds along Scott Crescent, past the towering spire of St Pauls, to the Gala Town Cross (circa 1599). A walk along Elm Row, Tea Street (by Whitchyknowe) and Glebe Street, all rich in local history, brings the walker onto Church Street and the former St Peter's School. At this point the way turns sharply left to explore Gala Aisle and the old burial ground of Galashiels (a list of grave markings can be obtained from Old Gala House).

Leave the Kirkyard by Bow Butts (an ancient archery practice ground), to reach the modern centre of the town, marked with statues of Sir Walter Scott, Robert Burns and Clapperton's "Border Reiver", then turn left to return to Old Gala House and light refreshments in the Pringle Room.

Walks in Gala Countryside *gives the visitor a taste of the Border hills and the silvery waters that enfold the town of Galashiels.*

The walks start from the public golf course, Mossilee and Hollybush Road, and are easily identified from *The Little Map of Gala.*

South of the town the terrain is relatively hilly and the walks utilise a section of the Southern Upland Way long distance path, covering the banks of the Tweed and the highest hill around Gala, Meigle Hill.

East via the Gala Water Valley could test the stamina of the walker, but this is compensated by the thoughtful route suggested and the many items of interest along the way. Items such as one of the three Pictish Brochs found in the Borders.

The walks to the west of Gala Water are both varied and testing, taking the walker to the lesser known corners of the steep sided hills and quiet valleys that lock this proud mill town well and truly into the centre of the Borders.

A WALK ROUND SELKIRK

The twenty page booklet, The Ring o the Toun, *is full of fascinating facts and illustrations about Selkirk. At 40p it can be obtained from the tourist information centre.*

Selkirk in Anglo-Saxon means "church in the forest", therefore the present name cannot have been in use before the 700s AD. Since then the town grew slowly, and as with all Border towns not always peacefully, with life centred around the Market Place now identified as "The Ring o the Toun". A triangle of streets, Kirk Wynd, Back Row (no reference to the rugby team), and High Street complete the ring, and are all included in the town trail. In the nineteenth century Selkirk expanded rapidly when the woollen trade boom hit the ancient burgh. With the aid of this 40p booklet the rich history of Selkirk and its characters become very much alive, and at no time more than during the annual celebrations of Common Riding

Week during July.

The trail begins and ends as all good town walks should, in the Market Place. First it goes to West Port, turning right to Kirk Wynd and then to Back Row, past the impressive Mungo Park Memorial in High Street, which it follows to the equally charismatic statue of Fletcher (the soul of Selkirk), at the Flodden Memorial. Here the walk turns to retrace its steps along High Street to the Market Place (with Sir Walter Scott in the centre). Leave the Market Place and walk down the Galashiels Road as far as the Sheriff Court and the Old Jail, then return to the starting point, the Market Place.

It is a walk that tells many stories of "Souters" great and small, of Fletcher, Walter Scott and Mungo Park, of Dr Lawson and Johnny Souter, James Hogg, and the Duke of Wellington (though not a Souter).

WALKS AROUND HAWICK

The small but informative booklet, Walks Around Hawick, *published by Hawick Community Council is available for 10p from the tourist information centre, situated in the Common Haugh car park. This sixteen page gem, complete with eight walks in and around the town, contains a map and a fund of local details and useful addresses and telephone numbers.*

Present day Hawick is the largest of the Scottish Border towns, with a population of 16,700, and is the undisputed capital of the Border knitwear industry. Unlike many of the other Border towns Hawick is perhaps not steeped so thoroughly in history and blood, yet in the words of Madge Elliot, "It is obvious this is a Mosstroopers Town." First recorded by the written word in a book about St Cuthbert in the twelfth century, and used extensively for many centuries as a staging post by the cattle drovers, it rose to prominence after Bailie John Hardie (1722-1800) brought the first knitting machines to Hawick, thus completing the tri-umvirate essential for a successful knitwear industry, sheep, water and machinery.

All the walks are circular, beginning and ending at the tourist information centre. They follow well defined paths and country lanes, with the routes well described.

WALK 1, Park, Trim-Track, Woods and Wilton Dean - A walk of 2¹/₂ miles close to the town centre, taking 1 hour to complete, but more enjoyable and longer in duration if the activities in the park are enjoyed.

WALK 2, Park and Riverside - An extension of Walk 1 to the extremities of the burgh boundary, taking a minimum time of $1^1/2$ hours.

WALK 3, Wellogate and Miller's Knowes Park - This is a short walk within the confines of the town, giving a birds-eye view of Hawick. 2 miles which should take no more than 1 hour to complete.

WALK 4, Loan, Moat Park, Longbaulk Track - With Hawick straddling the river Teviot most walks out of the town involve an ascent at some time and this is no exception, the distance of $2^1/4$ miles should take no longer than $1^1/4$ hours.

WALK 5, Loan, Crumhaughhill, Goldilands Tower - A longer walk this time, covering $4^1/2$ miles into the country and passing the sixteenth-century Border pele tower of Goldilands, once the property of Scotts of Buccleuch. This interesting stroll will last $2^1/2$ hours.

WALK 6, Loan, Crumhaughhill, Vertish Hill - $3^1/2$ miles including a section of walk 5 it offers a panoramic view of the entire town of Hawick. A camera would be an asset on this walk.

WALK 7, Loan, Vertish Hill, Williestruther Loch - Yet another out of town ramble of $4^1/2$ miles over the "Cornets Chase", used in the Common Riding ceremonies. A journey of $2^1/2$ hours.

WALK 8, Stirches, Dykeneuk, Whitehaugh, Wilton Dean - This walk embraces the peace of the Border countryside and enables the walker to enjoy the prominent landmarks of the Borders, such as Ruberslaw (the weathercock of Hawick), and The Cheviot, far away to the east. A walk of $4^1/2$ miles, taking $2^1/2$ hours to complete.

GLOSSARY

LOCAL TERMS AND NAMES

Bell -	Hill
Berwick cockles -	Very strong mint sweets
Bield -	Shelter, from the elements
Blaeberry -	Bilberry, small purple edible berry
Burn -	Small stream
Cairn -	Pile of stones or standing stone, route/burial site marker
Champian -	Level open country
Clagg -	Wet cloud/mist that suddenly envelopes summits
Cist -	Stone coffin
Clarts/Clarty -	Adhesive mud/muddy
Cleuch/Cleugh -	Narrow gully with burn, spellings as per OS maps
Col -	High saddle, lowest part of ridge between two summits
Common riding -	Riding town boundaries, an annual Border festival
Corrie -	Cirque or glaciated hollow in a mountainside
Craig -	Rocky crag/outcrop
Cushat -	Wood pigeon
Deer-hair -	Coarse grass on wet upland areas
Dod -	Surveyors' marker/pole. Also derivation of the name George
Doo -	Town pigeon
Dyke -	Dry stone wall, or man-made trench
Feral goat -	Wild goat descended from domestic stock
Gimmer -	Sheep ewe
Glar -	Mud
Glebe -	Church land, for grazing or cultivation
Glidders -	Scree (Northumbrian)
Haugh -	Flat ground by water
Hawick balls -	Strong round mint sweets
Heugh -	Sharp ended hill
Hole -	Hollow
Hope -	Sheltered valley
Jethart snails -	Mint flavoured sweets
Kames -	Glacial debris/ridges
Ken -	Know/understand
Knowe -	Small hill
Law -	Hill
Leat -	Water running to a mill

Linn -	Waterfall or waterslide
Loch -	Lake
Lochan -	Small lake
Lough -	Small lake (Northumbrian)
Moss trooper -	Young civic guard
Neb -	Nose
Nolt -	Cattle
Peewit -	Lapwing or plover
Reiver -	Cattle rustler or entrepreneur!
Rig* -	Ridge
Rill -	Small burn or stream
Scotch mist -	Low cloud and very wetting drizzle
Scotsman's heid -	Cotton grass, favours wet conditions
Scree -	Loose rocks/shale on the side of a hillside
Shiel -	Summer grazing, or a small hut on such ground
Spreat -	Species of rush
Steading -	Farm buildings/yard
Stell -	Round stone sheep shelter (Northumbrian)
Swire -	Neck of land
Syke -	Stream
Troots -	Trout
Trow -	Trough
Trows -	Little valleys
Tup -	Sheep, entire male/ram
Whaup -	Curlew
Wight -	Robust/manly

LOCAL PRONUNCIATIONS

Alwinton -	AL-INTON
Berwick -	BER-RIK
Bowerhope -	BIER-OP
Buccleuch -	BUCK-LOO
Hawick -	HOY-IK
Hownam -	HOO-NUM
Haugh -	HOFF OR HOCK
Jedburgh -	JED-BORO, known locally as JETHART
Cleuch -	CLOOK
Cleugh -	CLUFF
Lough -	LOFF

* Local spelling with one G, see OS maps of area.

BIBLIOGRAPHY

A Short Border History, Francis Hindes Groome (1887), J.&J.H.Rutherford, Kelso.

Border Poets, James Hogg, Sir Walter Scott.

Exploring Scotland's Heritage, Lothians and the Borders, Her Majesty's Stationery Office, Edinburgh.

Highways and Byways: in the Border, Andrew and John Lang, MacMillan and Co. London.

Homes and Haunts of Sir Walter Scott, George G.Napier (1897) J.MacLehose & Sons, Glasgow.

The Life of Sir Walter Scott, John Gibson Lockhart.

Pennine Way Companion, A.Wainwright, Michael Joseph, London.

Southern Upland Way, David Williams, Constable and Co. Ltd, London.

The Border Line, James Logan Mack, Edinburgh.

The Borders, F.R.Banks, B.T.Batsford, London.

The Drove Roads of Scotland, A.R.B.Haldane.

The Southern Uplands, Andrew & Thrippleton, Scottish Mountaineering Council.

The Steel Bonnets, George MacDonald Fraser, Barrie and Jenkins Ltd 1971, and Collins 1989 (paperback).

Walks in the Cheviot Hills, Northumberland County Council, National Park and Countryside Department, Hexham.

USEFUL INFORMATION

ACCOMMODATION

Lists and bookings together with a Book-a-Bed-Ahead scheme, plus details of transport, border abbeys, castles, ancient monuments, museums and galleries, visitors' centres, gardens, crafts, leisure and recreation, and 'What's On' can be obtained from the tourist information centres listed below: -

Scottish Borders Tourist Board

Coldstream, Henderson Park, open April-October - (0890) 2607
Eyemouth, Auld Kirk, open April-October - (08907) 50678
Galashiels, Bank Street, open April-October - (0896) 55551
Hawick, Common Haugh, open April-October - (0450) 72547
Jedburgh, Murrays Green, open all year - (0835) 63688
Kelso, Town House, open April-October - (0573) 223464
Melrose, Priorwood Gardens, open April-October - (089682) 2555
Peebles, Chambers Institute, open April-October - (0721) 20138
Selkirk, Halliwells House, open April-October - (0750) 20054

Northumbria Tourist Board

Aykley Heads, Durham DH1 5UX -	(091) 3846905
Tourist Information Centre, Castlegate, Berwick-upon-Tweed -	(0289) 330733
Tourist Information Centre, High Street Car Park, Wooler -	(0668) 81602

Scottish Youth Hostels

Abbey St Bathans, Duns, open 15/5-29/10 -	(03614) 217
Broadmeadows, Old Brodmeadows, Selkirk, open 29/3-30/9 -	(075076) 262
Coldingham, The Mount, Coldingham, open 29/3-30/9 -	(08907) 71298
Kirk Yetholm, The Green, Kirk Yetholm, Kelso, open 22/3-30/9 -	
	(057382) 631
Melrose, Priorwood, Melrose, open 1/3-30/9 -	(089682) 2521
Snoot, Roberton, Hawick, open 29/3-30/9 -	(045088) 224

English Youth Hostels

Byrness, 18 South Green, Byrness, open Mar-Sept -	(0830) 20222
Wooler, Cheviot Road, Wooler, open Mar-Sept -	(0668) 81365

TRANSPORT

Air

Edinburgh International Airport, Turnhouse, Edinburgh -	(031) 333 1000
Newcastle International Airport, Woolsington, Newcastle upon Tyne -	
	(091) 2860966

Rail

British Rail, Berwick-upon-Tweed -	(0289) 306771
Scot Rail, Waverley Station, Edinburgh -	(031) 556 2477
British Rail, Carlisle -	(0228) 44711

Road, Long Distance

National Express Ltd, Galloway Coach Station, Newcastle upon Tyne -
(091) 261 9727

Scottish Citylink Coaches Ltd. Buchanan Bus Station, Killermont Street, Glasgow:

Glasgow	(041) 332 9191
Edinburgh	(031) 557 5717
London	(071) 636 9373
Galashiels	(0896) 2237

Caledonian Express Ltd, Walnut Grove, Perth PH2 7LP:

Edinburgh	(031) 452 8777
Glasgow	(041) 332 4100
London	(071) 730 0202

Local Services
Timetables and fare details available from:
Director of Roads and Transportation, Borders Regional Council
Newtown St Boswells, Melrose, Roxburghshire TD6 0SA -   (0835) 23301
Berwick upon Tweed Bus Station, Main Street, Berwick.
    Lowland Scottish -   (0289) 307461
    Northumbria -   (0289) 307283

MISCELLANEOUS ADDRESSES
British Mountaineering Council, Crawford House, Precinct Centre, Booth Street East, Manchester M13 9RZ
Countryside Commission for Scotland, Battleby, Redgorton, Perth PH1 3EW
Countryside Ranger Service, Borders Regional Council, Newtown St Boswells, Melrose TD6 0SA
Forestry Commission Headquarters, 231 Corstorphine Road, Edinburgh EH12 7AT
Long Distance Walkers' Association, 29 Marway Road, Brotton, Saltburn-by-Sea, Cleveland TS12 2RH
Mountaineering Council of Scotland, National Officer, Flat 1R, 71 King Street, Crieff, Perthshire, PH7 3HB
National Trust, 36 Queen Anne's Gate, London SW1H 9AS
Nature Conservancy Council, Archbold House, Archbold Terrace, Newcastle upon Tyne, NE2 1EG
Northumberland National Park, Eastburn, South Park, Hexham, Northumberland - (0434) 605555
Ordnance Survey, Romsey Road, Maybush, Southampton, SO9 4DH; a range of local OS maps available from local out-door shops and newsagents.
Ramblers' Association, 1/5, Wandsworth Road, London SW8 2LJ
Royal Society for the Protection of Birds, The Lodge, Sandy, Beds SG19 2DL
Scottish Rights of Way Society, 29 Rutland Place, Edinburgh EH1 2BW
Scottish Youth Hostels Association, 7 Glebe Crescent, Stirling FK8 2JA
Woodland Trust, Westgate, Grantham, Lincs NG31 6LL
Youth Hostels Association, Trevelyan House, St Albans, Herts AL1 2DY

Mountain Rescue Services/Police - Freephone Dial 999

Borders General Hospital, Huntlyburn Melrose, Roxburghshire. Tel-
(0896) 4333

WEATHER FORECASTS:
(1) Newcastle Meteorological Office, Newcastle Weather Centre, for the Cheviot Hills -   (091) 232 6453
(2) Glasgow Weather Centre, for the Southern Uplands and the Tweed Valley -   (041) 248 3451
(3) Edinburgh Meteorological Office, Edinburgh Weather Centre -
                                                                    (031) 244 8362/8363
(4) Mountain Call, Eastern Borders -   (0898) 500 422
(5) Weather Watchers, any area -   (06445) 652 4239
(6) Daily forecasts, Radio Borders, FM 96.8
(7) Daily forecasts, Border Television, Teletext page 183
(8) Scottish Road Weather Line -   (0898) 567 598

✳   ✳   ✳

223

PRINTED BY
CARNMOR PRINT & DESIGN, LONDON ROAD, PRESTON